Foreword

MW01614423

The *Daily Mental Math* series has been designed to help students improve both their speed of recall of important mathematical facts and terminology as they progress through Grades 8–10.

Most adults choose mental methods when calculating in their daily lives. To provide a reason to calculate, many questions in this series have been posed in real-life contexts. The context in which a question is posed will also help students to judge the reasonableness of their answer.

Four days of mental math questions have been provided for each week, since this fits most school schedules. Daily practice of around 10–15 minutes is highly recommended. The emphasis should first be on building accuracy and then on improving speed.

The questions for each day have been organized so that similar types of questions are presented together. Each concept is introduced within a framework of repetitive questions with slight variations to help students become familiar with the patterns and relationships that occur for that concept. Some items are presented alongside their inverses to highlight the relationships between concepts; for example, $\sqrt{625} = \square$ and $25^2 = \square$.

Used daily, the *Daily Mental Math* series gives students the practice they need to develop strong mental math and problem-solving skills.

Contents

Day 1

1. $\sqrt{0.81}$ = _____

2. 0.9 + 0.09 = _____

3. 0.9 − 0.09 = _____

4. 0.9 × 0.09 = _____

5. 0.9 ÷ 0.09 = _____

6. Draw a **prime factor tree** for the number 12.

7. The **symbol** for **millionths** is _____.

8. How many **square meters** are there in a two-meter-by-two-meter **square**? _____

9. Part of a circle that can be drawn without lifting a pencil is called an _____.

10. 3 cm = _____ mm

11. How many **milliseconds** are there in one second?

    _____

12. When a circle shape is cut from a **cone,** it is called a c_____ section.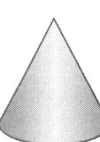

13. How many **sides** does a **rhombus** have? _____

14. $3 ÷ $0.25 = _____

15. How many **years** are there in a **century**? _____

16. 23 + 29 = _____

17. Find the **cost** of 15 hamburgers at $2.85 each.

    _____

18. Express 1962 in **Roman numerals.**

    _____

19. How many **kilometers** are there in a **nautical mile?**

    _____

20. $9^2 - 7^2$ = _____

Day 2

1. 0.9^2 = _____

2. 0.9 + 0.08 = _____

3. 0.9 − 0.08 = _____

4. 0.9 × 0.08 = _____

5. Express 0.9 ÷ 0.08 as a **fraction.** _____

6. Draw a different **prime factor tree** for 12.

7. A **half line** is called a _____.

8. How many **square feet** are there in a one-foot-by-one-foot **square**?

    _____

9. The **symbol** for **micro** is _____.

10. 200 cm = _____ m

11. How many **millimeters** in one meter? _____

12. What happens to water when its **temperature** reaches 100°C? _____

13. How many **sides** does a **nonagon** have?

    _____

14. $3 ÷ $0.15 = _____

15. How many **years** does a **bicentennial** commemorate? _____

16. 24 + 28 = _____

17. Find the **cost** of 14 hamburgers at $2.95 each.

    _____

18. Express 1961 in **Roman numerals.**

    _____

19. How many **kilometers** will a boat travel in an hour if it is traveling at **one knot?**

    _____

20. $8^2 - 5^2$ = _____

Score: _____ /20 _____ %

Score: _____ /20 _____ %

Week 1

Day 3

1. $\sqrt{0.49}$ = _____

2. $0.9 + 0.07$ = _____

3. $0.9 - 0.07$ = _____

4. 0.9×0.07 = _____

5. Express $0.9 \div 0.07$ as a **fraction**. _____

6. If all **points** are on the same **plane**, they are cop_____.

7. Are 10, 24, and 26 a **Pythagorean triple?** Yes No

8. How many **square meters** are there in a three-meter-by-three-meter **square**? _____

9. If Lianni **saves** $24 per week, how much does she save in a year?

   _____

10. $^3/_4$ m = _____ cm

11. What is the tenth number in this **sequence**?

    4, 10, 16, 22, … , _____

12. A **fixed quantity** is called a c_____.

13. How many **sides** does a **kite** have? _____

14. If Lauren's heart beats 68 times per minute, how many times does it beat in one hour?

    _____

15. $25 + 27$ = _____

16. How many **square meters** is a **hectare**?

    _____

17. If Pietro's **average** after three tests is 88%, what must he score on his next test to make his **average** 90%?

    _____

18. Express 1957 in **Roman numerals**.

    _____

19. $2^2 \times 10$ = _____

20. How many **dozen** are there in 12? _____

Day 4

1. 0.7^2 = _____

2. $0.9 + 0.06$ = _____

3. $0.9 - 0.06$ = _____

4. 0.9×0.06 = _____

5. Express $0.9 \div 0.06$ as a **simplified fraction**.

   _____

6. A **decagon** is a _____-sided 2-D shape.

7. Are 7, 24, and 25 a **Pythagorean triple?** Yes No

8. Draw a **hyperbola**.

9. If Lianni **saves** $30 per week, how much does she save in a year? _____

10. One thousand, five hundred **meters** is _____ km.

11. The **prime factors** of 69 are _____.

12. An example of something **finite** is _____

    _____.

13. How many **sides** does a **chevron** have? _____

14. How many **years** are there in a **sesquicentennial?** _____

15. $360 \div 9$ = _____

16. How many square meters are there in a **hectare?** _____

17. How many games has the soccer team played if the team is $^3/_4$ of the way into the season with five games left to play?

    _____

18. Express 1964 in **Roman numerals**.

    _____

19. Find the **reciprocal** of 0.3. _____

20. How many **dozen** are there in 24? _____

Score: ____ /20   ____ %   Score: ____ /20   ____ %

Week 2

Day 1

1. $0.8^2 =$ _____0.64_____

2. $0.9 + 0.05 =$ _____

3. $0.9 - 0.05 =$ _____

4. $0.9 \times 0.05 =$ _____

5. $0.9 \div 0.05 =$ _____

6. An **angle** is formed when two r_adius_ join at a **vertex**.

7. Are 5, 12, and 13 a **Pythagorean triple**?   Yes   (No)

8. How many **square feet** are there in a four-foot-by-four-foot **square**? ____16____

9. How many **milligrams** is one gram? _____

10. 1750 m = _____ km

11. Rewrite 0.245×10^3 in **regular notation**.
    _____245_____

12. An example of something **infinite** is __Pi__
    _____.

13. A **decagon** has ____10____ sides and is a _____-dimensional shape.

14. The **prime factors** of 87 are __3, 29__.

15. **Half** of 132 is ____66____.

16. If the **product** of a number and 1.5 is 7.5, what is the number?
    _____6_____

17. If Audrey's **average** after three tests is 68%, what must she score on her next test to make her average 70%?
    _____80%_____

18. Express 1970 in **Roman numerals**.
    _____

19. $3 - 0.5 =$ _____2.5_____

20. Is a set of **negative numbers** finite or infinite?
    (a) finite   (b) infinite

Day 2

1. $\sqrt{0.64} =$ _____

2. $0.9 + 0.04 =$ _____

3. $0.9 - 0.04 =$ _____

4. $0.9 \times 0.04 =$ _____

5. Express $0.9 \div 0.4$ as a **fraction**. _____

6. What does the scale **degrees Celsius** measure? _____

7. Are 14, 48, and 50 a **Pythagorean triple**?   Yes   No

8. How many **square feet** are there in a five-foot-by-five-foot **square**?
   _____

9. How many **milliliters** is one liter? _____

10. 2250 m = _____ km

11. Rewrite 0.345×10^2 in **conventional notation**.
    _____

12. An **angle** is two **rays** joined at a v_____.

13. A **decahedron** has _____ sides and is a _____-dimensional shape.

14. The **prime factors** of 70 are _____.

15. **Double** 39. _____

16. If the **product** of a number and 1.2 is 0.96, what is the number?
    _____

17. If $^2/_3$ of an amount is 50, what is the amount?
    _____

18. Express 1958 in **Roman numerals**.
    _____

19. $4 - 0.6 =$ _____

20. Is the set of **decimal numbers** between 1.4 and 1.5 finite or infinite?
    (a) finite   (b) infinite

Score: _____ /20   _____%   Score: _____ /20   _____%

Day 3

1. $\sqrt{0.01}$ = _____

2. $0.9 + 0.03$ = _____

3. $0.9 - 0.03$ = _____

4. 0.9×0.03 = _____

5. $0.9 \div 0.03$ = _____

6. If Storm runs 100 m in 10 seconds, what is her **speed** in km/h? _____

7. **Increase** $500 by 12%. _____

8. How many **square feet** are there in a six-foot-by-six-foot **square**? _____

9. $^3/_4 \times$ _____ = 6

10. 3750 m = _____ km

11. In geometry, a **path** that can be drawn in a plane without lifting a pencil is called a

    c_____.

12. Correct 0.00456 to three decimal places. _____

13. Name a **quadrilateral** with both pairs of sides parallel.

    _____

14. $81^{1/2}$ = _____

15. A **quarter** of 120 is _____.

16. Find the tenth number in the **sequence**.

    19, 18, 17, … , _____

17. Chandra buys two raffle tickets. If 500 tickets were sold, what are his **chances** of winning?

    _____

18. Express 1953 in **Roman numerals**.

    _____

19. Which of the **angles** in a **rhombus** are equal in size?

    (a) all four

    (b) the diagonal angles

    (c) none

20. $5 - 0.7$ = _____

Score: /20   %

Day 4

1. 0.1^2 = _____

2. $0.9 + 0.02$ = _____

3. $0.9 - 0.02$ = _____

4. 0.9×0.02 = _____

5. $0.9 \div 0.02$ = _____

6. Half of **three and a half million dollars** is

    _____.

7. Which number **divided** by 0.2 results in 10? _____

8. How many **square feet** are there in a seven-foot-by-seven-foot **square**? _____

9. Two-thirds of _____ = 12

10. 1 ha = _____ m²

11. The number of hours students spend watching television could be shown on a

    f_____ g_____.

12. Correct 0.00789 to three decimal places. _____

13. A **polygon** with four sides is known as a

    _____

14. $8^{1/3}$ = _____

15. How many bags of 30 sweets can be made with 150 sweets? _____

16. Find the tenth number in the **sequence**.

    19, 18.5, 18, … , _____

17. James buys four tickets in a raffle. If his chances of winning are $^1/_{125}$, how many tickets have been sold? _____

18. Express 1947 in **Roman numerals**.

    _____

19. Which sides of a **rhombus** are equal in length?

    (a) all four

    (b) the opposite pairs

20. $6 - 0.8$ = _____

Score: /20   %

Day 1

1. $\sqrt{1.21}$ = _____

2. 0.9 + 0.01 = _____

3. 0.9 − 0.01 = _____

4. 0.9 × 0.01 = _____

5. 0.9 ÷ 0.01 = _____

6. Driving at 90 km/h, Rory notices he has six kilometers more to drive before he exits the freeway. How long will this take?

   _____

7. During a 35%-off book sale, how much would a $14 book **cost**?

   _____

8. How many **square feet** are there in an eight foot-by-eight foot **square**? _____

9. $^2/_3$ × _____ = 14

10. 500 g = _____ kg

11. Correct 0.00123 to three decimal places.

    _____

12. The **prime factors** of 42 are _____ .

13. A **quadrilateral** with two pairs of parallel sides that are also congruent is called a

    _____ .

14. What **type** of graph is this?

    _____

15. What **fraction** of a second is a **millisecond**?

    _____

16. Find the tenth number in the **sequence**.

    19, 16.5, 14, … , _____

17. 150 ÷ 30 = _____

18. The **inverse** of **multiplication** is

    d_____ .

19. 6.65% written as a **decimal** is _____

20. 7 − 0.9 = _____

Day 2

1. 1.1^2 = _____

2. 0.9 + 0.001 = _____

3. 0.9 − 0.001 = _____

4. 0.9 × 0.001 = _____

5. 0.9 ÷ 0.001 = _____

6. Driving at 80 km/h, Caitlin notices she has four kilometers more to drive before she exits the freeway. How long will this take?

   _____

7. During a 35%-off book sale, how much would a $24 book **cost**?

   _____

8. How many **square feet** are there in a nine foot-by-nine foot **square**? _____

9. $^3/_4$ × _____ = 12

10. 21,750 g = _____ kg

11. Correct 0.00452 to three decimal places.

    _____

12. The **prime factors** of 84 are _____ .

13. A **quadrilateral** with perpendicular diagonals of which the shorter is **bisected** is called a

    _____ .

14. The shape in this graph

    is a p_____ .

    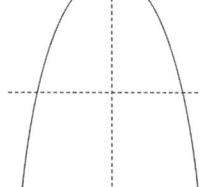

15. What **fraction** of a meter is a **millimeter**?

    _____

16. Find the tenth number in the **sequence**.

    19, 17.5, 16, … , _____

17. 160 ÷ 40 = _____

18. The inverse of **addition** is

    s_____ .

19. $6^2/_3$% written as a **decimal** is _____ .

20. 8 − 1.01 = _____

Day 3

1. $\sqrt{1.44}$ = _____

2. $0.8 + 0.01$ = _____

3. $0.8 - 0.01$ = _____

4. 0.8×0.01 = _____

5. $0.8 \div 0.01$ = _____

6. How many plants are needed for a 10 ft-long hedge if they are to be planted 0.5 ft apart?

   _____

7. Today's date in **international standard date** notation is _YYYY_ / _MM_ / _DD_ .

8. How many **square feet** are there in a 10 foot-by-10 foot **square**? _____

9. $^1/_2 \times$ _____ = 10

10. What **fraction** of one dollar is one cent? _____

11. Correct 0.00455 to three decimal places.

    _____

12. The **prime factors** of 16 are _____.

13. Another term for a **tessellation** is t _____.

14. Which is the **largest**?
    (a) 24%   (b) $^1/_4$ (c) 0.026   (d) $^{13}/_{48}$

15. What **fraction** of a meter is a **centimeter**?

    _____

16. If the **average** of four scores is 42, what is the **total** of the scores? _____

17. **Sixteen** written as a **power** is _____.

18. **Repeated addition** is the same as m_____.

19. If Adele's **average** after three tests is 75%, what must she score on her next test to make her average 76%?

    _____

20. $35 - 0.5$ = _____

Day 4

1. 1.2^2 = _____

2. $0.8 + 0.02$ = _____

3. $0.8 - 0.02$ = _____

4. 0.8×0.02 = _____

5. $0.8 \div 0.02$ = _____

6. How many fence posts are needed for a 10 foot-long fence if they are to be one foot apart?

   _____

7. During a 35%-off book sale, how much would a $15 book cost? _____

8. How many **square feet** are there in an 11 foot-by-11 foot **square**? _____

9. 0.5 of _____ = 7.5

10. One day of one week, as a **fraction**, is _____.

11. Correct 0.00456 to three decimal places. _____

12. The **prime factors** of eight are _____.

13. How many equal-length **diagonals** are there in a **rectangle**? _____

14. Which is the **largest**?
    (a) 23%   (b) $^1/_5$ (c) 0.24   (d) $^{12}/_{48}$

15. What **fraction** of a liter is a **milliliter**?

    _____

16. If the **average** of five scores is 36, what is the **total** of the scores?

    _____

17. **Eight** written as a **power** is _____.

18. **Repeated subtraction** is the same as d_____.

19. If Hamlet's **average** after three tests is 72%, what must he score on his next test to make his average 75%?

    _____

20. $40 - 0.6$ = _____

Week 4

Day 1

1. $\sqrt{0.09}$ = _____   2. $0.8 + 0.03$ = _____

3. $0.8 - 0.04$ = _____

4. 0.8×0.03 = _____

5. $0.8 \div 0.03$ (as a **fraction**) = _____

6. Find the **volume** of this **solid**.
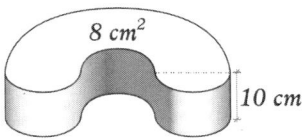

   _____

7. Bill was first voted class president for the year four years ago, so this is his _____th election as president.

8. How many **square feet** are there in a 12 foot-by-12 foot **square**? _____

9. $\frac{1}{10} \times$ _____ $= 30$

10. 200 g of 1 kg as a **fraction** is _____.

11. What is the **value** of a on this **number line**?

    _____

12. Correct 0.00446 to three decimal places.

    _____

13. The name for a **symmetrical trapezoid** is

    _____.
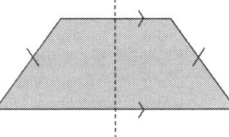

14. **Twenty-five percent** is equal to _____ parts out of 12.

15. What year is MMXVII in **Arabic** (standard) **numerals**?

    _____

16. The **width** of a **circle** is called the

    d_____.

17. Name something that might be a **hectare** in size.

    _____

18. Another term for **width** is b_____.

19. $30 + 0.05$ = _____

20. The **cube root** of 64 is _____.

Score: _____ /20 _____ %

Day 2

1. 0.3^2 = _____   2. $0.8 + 0.04$ = _____

3. $0.8 - 0.04$ = _____

4. 0.8×0.04 = _____

5. $0.8 \div 0.04$ = _____

6. Find the **volume** of this solid.
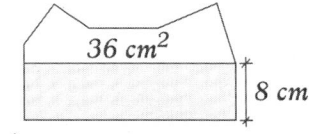

   _____

7. If Carly has just been elected annual president of her club for the sixth time, how many years have passed since she was first elected? _____

8. How many **square feet** are there in a 13 foot-by-13 foot **square**? _____

9. $\frac{1}{100} \times$ _____ $= 4$

10. 500 g of 1 kg as a **fraction** is _____.

11. What is the **value** of t on this **number line**?
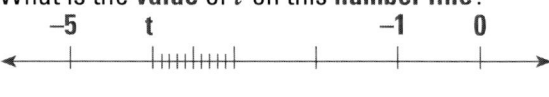

    _____

12. Correct 0.00416 to three decimal places.

    _____

13. A **network** with a path that includes each edge exactly once is called a

    t_____ n_____.

14. What **unit** is used to measure boat speeds?

    _____

15. What year is MMXVIII in **Arabic** (standard) **numerals**? _____

16. Half the **width** of a **circle** is called the r_____.

17. If the **average** of four scores is 36, what is the **total** of the scores? _____

18. Name something that might weigh a **ton**.

    _____

19. $4.2 + 0.06$ = _____

20. $\sqrt[3]{64}$ = _____

Score: _____ /20 _____ %

Week 4

Day 3

1. $\sqrt{0.36} =$ _____
2. $0.8 + 0.05 =$ _____
3. $0.8 - 0.05 =$ _____
4. $0.8 \times 0.05 =$ _____
5. $0.8 \div 0.05 =$ _____
6. Find the **volume** of this **irregular solid**.

   _____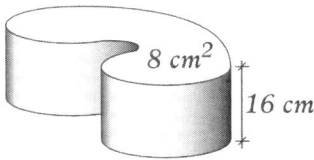

7. Today's date in **international standard date** notation is _____ / _____ / _____ .
8. How many **square feet** are there in a 15 foot-by-15 foot **square**? _____
9. $^3/_4 \times$ _____ $= 12$
10. Five minutes as a **fraction** of one hour is _____ .
11. What is the **value** of a on this **number line**?

    -8 -6 a 0

    _____

12. Correct 0.00456 to four decimal places. _____
13. A fourth of a circular region, formed when two **radii** are at right angles, is a _____ .
14. What is the **outlier** in this set of scores: 64, 65, 65, 66, 69, 100? _____
15. **Twenty-five percent** is equal to three parts out of _____ .
16. If the **average** of four scores is 4.4, what is the **total** of the scores? _____
17. **Celsius** is a measurement unit for t_____
18. On what date does winter begin?

    _____ .

19. If Nick's **average** after three tests is 80%, what must he score on his next test to make his average 85%? _____
20. $43.08 - 0.5 =$ _____

Day 4

1. $0.6^2 =$ _____
2. $0.8 + 0.06 =$ _____
3. $0.8 - 0.06 =$ _____
4. $0.8 \times 0.06 =$ _____
5. $0.8 \div 0.06$ (as a **fraction**) $=$ _____
6. Find the **volume** of this **irregular solid**.

   _____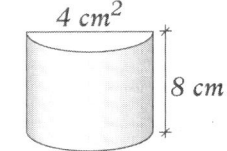

7. During a 35%-off book sale, how much would a $16 book cost? _____
8. How many **square feet** are there in a 100 foot-by-100 foot **square**? _____
9. $^3/_4 \times$ _____ $= 15$
10. Take $^1/_6$ from $1^1/_2$. _____
11. What is the **value** of a on this **number line**?

    0 2 4 a 8

    _____

12. Correct 0.00496 to four decimal places. _____
13. A **plane** region between two **concentric circles** is an _____ .
14. What is the **outlier** in this set of data: 2, 11, 12, 13, 14? _____ .
15. **Fifty percent** is equal to three parts out of _____ .
16. If the **average** of four scores is 402, what is the **sum** of the scores? _____
17. **Altitude** is a measure of _____ .
18. On what date does summer begin?

    _____ .

19. If Roy's **average** after three tests is 62%, what must he score on his next test to make his average 65%? _____
20. $42.8 - 0.6 =$ _____

Day 1

1. $\sqrt{0.25}$ = _____

2. 0.8 + 0.07 = _____

3. 0.8 − 0.07 = _____

4. 0.8 × 0.07 = _____

5. 0.8 ÷ 0.07 (as a fraction) = _____

6. Find the **perimeter** of this **triangle**.

   _____

   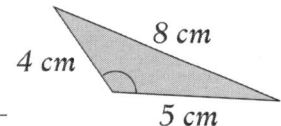

7. Find the value of $\sqrt{(-4)^2 + (-3)^2}$.

   _____

8. What might be measured in **micrometers** (μm)?

   _____

9. $^3/_4 \times$ _____ = 36

10. What is 50% of 564? _____

11. Correct 0.01406 to three decimal places.

    _____

12. A 3-D **annulus** is a _____.

13. **Seventy-five percent** is equal to three parts out of _____.

14. How many **minutes** are there in a **degree**?

    _____

15. A **set** within a set is called a _____.

16. If the **average** of six scores is 42, what is the **total** of the scores?

    _____

17. If 16 is a **square number**, what might another square number be?

    _____

18. On what date does fall begin?

    _____.

19. How many **dozen** are there in 36?

    _____

20. 36.05 − 0.5 = _____

Day 2

1. 0.5^2 = _____

2. 0.8 + 0.08 = _____

3. 0.8 − 0.08 = _____

4. 0.8 × 0.08 = _____

5. 0.8 ÷ 0.08 = _____

6. Find the **perimeter** of this **triangle**. _____

   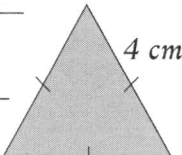

7. Find the value of $\sqrt{(-5)^2 + (-12)^2}$.

   _____

8. What might be measured in **millimeters**?

   _____

9. $^3/_4 \times$ _____ = 21

10. What is $^7/_{10}$ of 1360? _____

11. Correct 0.00479 to three decimal places.

    _____

12. $^1/_1$ as a **decimal** is _____.

13. **Ten percent** is equal to one part out of _____.

14. What **unit** is used to measure **sound intensity level** (loudness)?

    _____

15. The **apex** is an object's

    _____ v_____.

16. If the **average** of seven scores is 42, what is the **total** of the scores?

    _____

17. If 27 is a **cubed number**, what might another cubed number be?

    _____

18. On what date does spring begin?

    _____.

19. How many **dozen** are there in 48? _____

20. 40 − 0.6 = _____

Score:	/20	%	Score:	/20	%

Day 3

1. $\sqrt{0.0625}$ = _____

2. 0.8 + 0.09 = _____

3. 0.8 − 0.09 = _____

4. 0.8 × 0.09 = _____

5. 0.8 ÷ 0.09 (as a **fraction**) = _____

6. Find the **perimeter** of this **triangle**.

   _____

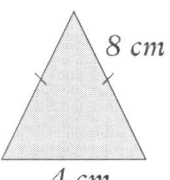
8 cm
4 cm

7. From the **sum** of −7 and −5, and **subtract** the **product** of −2 and −6. _____

8. If Hugh **saves** $35 per week, how much is this per year? _____

9. What might be measured in **grams**?

   _____

10. $3\frac{1}{2} - \frac{5}{8}$ = _____

11. What is the **value** of a on this **number line**?

    _____

0   a 12

12. $\frac{1}{1}$ as a **percentage** is _____.

13. **Ten percent** is equal to _____ parts out of 100.

14. If Samantha **bought** bank shares for $20 and **sold** them for $25, what percentage of the original cost is her **profit**? _____

15. What **fraction** of a **hectare** is 1 m²? _____

16. If the **average** of eight scores is 42, what is the **total** of the scores? _____

17. What **fraction** of a **pound** is an **ounce**? _____

18. What **unit** can be used to measure gale force **wind speed**? _____

19. If Mitchell's three-test **average** is 71%, what must he score on his next test to make his average 75%?

    _____

20. How many **dozen** are there in 60? _____

Score: _____ /20 _____ %

Day 4

1. 0.25^2 = _____

2. 0.08 + 0.09 = _____

3. 0.08 − 0.09 = _____

4. 0.08 × 0.09 = _____

5. 0.08 ÷ 0.09 (as a **fraction**) = _____

6. Find the **perimeter** of this **triangle**.

   _____

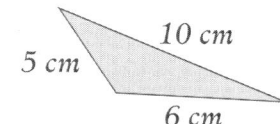
10 cm
5 cm
6 cm

7. From the **sum** of −9 and −7, and **subtract** the **product** of −2 and −3. _____

8. If Hugo **saves** $45 per week, how much is this per year? _____

9. What might be measured in **kiloliters**?

   _____

10. $\frac{3}{8}$ of 488 = _____

11. What is the **value** of a on this **number line**?

    _____

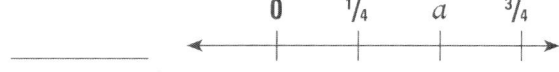
0    $\frac{1}{4}$ a $\frac{3}{4}$

12. $\frac{1}{1}$ as a **ratio** is _____.

13. **Ten percent** is equal to _____ parts out of 200.

14. If Douglas **bought** mining company shares for $2 and **sold** them for $10, what percentage of the original price is his **profit**? _____

15. How many ft² are there in an **acre**? _____

16. If the **average** of nine scores is 42, what is the **total** of the scores? _____

17. What **fraction** of a **foot** is an **inch**? _____

18. The **circumference** of the Earth is _____ **nautical miles**. (Hint: Think of the relationship among circle, degree, and minute.)

19. If Andrew's **average** after three tests is 55%, what must he score on his next test to raise his average to 60%? _____

20. How many **dozen** are there in 72? _____

Score: _____ /20 _____ %

Day 1

1. $\sqrt{0.16}$ = _____
2. 0.7 + 0.01 = _____
3. 0.7 − 0.01 = _____
4. 0.7 × 0.01 = _____
5. 0.7 ÷ 0.01 = _____
6. What is the **largest customary unit** for measuring water? _____
7. From the **sum** of −8 and −9, **subtract** the **product** of −2 and −6. _____
8. If Lianni **saves** $50 per week, how much is this per year? _____
9. What might be measured in **megaliters**?

   _____
10. 40,408 × 25 = _____
11. Write an **inequality** for the **value** of y on this **number line**.

    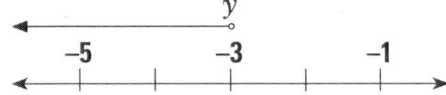

    _____
12. $^1/_2$ as a **percentage** is _____.
13. **Ten percent** is equal to _____ parts out of 20.
14. If Dean **bought** mining company shares for $0.20 and **sold** them for $0.80, what percentage of the original price is his **profit**? _____
15. What **fraction** of a **kilometer** is a **millimeter**?

    _____
16. If the **average** of three scores is 42, what is the **total** of the scores? _____
17. A **mathematical rule** expressed with symbols is called a f_____.
18. Which is **greater**? (a) 7.65% (b) 7$^2/_3$%
19. How many **dozen** are there in 84? _____
20. 3.5 ÷ 0.1 = _____

Day 2

1. 0.4^2 = _____ 2. 0.7 + 0.02 = _____
3. 0.7 − 0.02 = _____
4. 0.7 × 0.02 = _____
5. 0.7 ÷ 0.02 = _____
6. Find the **perimeter** of this **triangle**.

   _____

   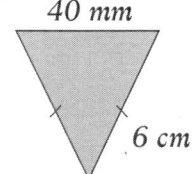
   40 mm
   6 cm
7. From the **sum** of −8 and −5, and **subtract** the **product** of −3 and −4. _____
8. If Liam **saves** $55 per week, how much is this per year? _____
9. What is the **largest metric unit** for measuring water? _____
10. 848,164 × 25 = _____
11. Write an **inequality** for the **value** of b on this **number line**.

    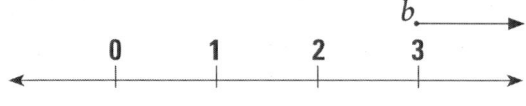

    _____
12. $^1/_2$ as a **decimal** is _____.
13. **Ten percent** is equal to _____ parts out of 2000.
14. If Dale **bought** mining company shares for $1 and **sold** them for $1.50, what percentage of the original price is his **profit**? _____
15. The **size** of the **surface** of an object is known as its a_____.
16. If the **average** of two scores is 42, what is the **total** of the scores? _____
17. A **vertical bar graph** with no space between successive bars is called a h_____.
18. How much **annual interest** is paid on $2000 at 7.25% for a year? _____
19. How many **dozen** are there in 96? _____
20. 4.5 ÷ 0.9 = _____

Day 3

1. Evaluate 1^{-1}. _____
2. $0.7 + 0.03 =$ _____
3. $0.7 - 0.03 =$ _____
4. $0.7 \times 0.03 =$ _____
5. $0.7 \div 0.03$ (as a fraction) = _____
6. Find the **perimeter** of this **triangle**.

   _____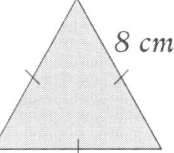

   8 cm

7. To the **sum** of −9 and −5, **add** the **product** of −2 and −4. _____
8. If Amalie **saves** $50 per week, how much is this per year? _____
9. What **unit of mass** might the amount of a vitamin in a food be measured in? _____
10. What **fraction** is exactly halfway between $^1/_2$ and $^1/_4$? _____
11. $13 \div 0.1 =$ _____
12. $^1/_2$ as a **ratio** is _____.
13. **Ten percent** is equal to _____ parts out of 60.
14. Two or more **circles** that share the same **center** are _____.
15. Another term for a **circular prism** is a c_____.
16. The _____ of a line is its rate of change.
17. The **product** of any number and one is always that _____.
18. If Dot **bought** mining company shares for $2 and **sold** them for $1, what percentage of the original price is her **loss**?

    _____
19. How many **dozen** are there in 108? _____
20. The **cube root** of 125 is _____.

Score: _____ /20 _____ %

Day 4

1. $1.5^2 =$ _____
2. $0.7 + 0.04 =$ _____
3. $0.7 - 0.04 =$ _____
4. $0.7 \times 0.04 =$ _____
5. $0.7 \div 0.04$ (as a fraction) = _____
6. Find the **perimeter** of this **triangle**.

   _____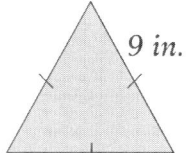

   9 in.

7. To the **sum** of −3 and −5, **add** the **product** of −2 and −3. _____
8. If Cary **saves** $52 per week, how much is this per year? _____
9. What **unit of mass** might be used to compare the weights of trucks? _____
10. What **fraction** lies halfway between $^1/_2$ and $^3/_4$?

    _____
11. $12.5 \times 0.1 =$ _____
12. $^3/_4$ as a **percentage** is _____.
13. **Ten percent** is equal to _____ parts out of 600.
14. Half a circular region formed by the circle's **diameter** and half of the **circle** is a

    _____.
15. Another term for **multiplicative inverse** is r_____.
16. Another term for **slope** is g_____.
17. Another term for the **intersection** of a network of **paths** is called a n_____.
18. What is Earth's **circumference** in km? *(Use 1.85 km = 1 nm and C = 21,600 nautical miles.)*

    _____
19. How many **dozen** are there in 120? _____
20. $\sqrt[3]{125} =$ _____

Score: _____ /20 _____ %

Week 7

Day 1

1. Evaluate 2^{-1}. _____

2. $0.7 + 0.05 =$ _____

3. $0.7 - 0.05 =$ _____

4. $0.7 \times 0.05 =$ _____

5. Write $0.7 \div 0.05$ as a **simplified fraction**. _____

6. Find the **perimeter** of this **triangle**. _____

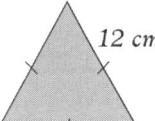
12 cm

7. To the **sum** of -5 and -11, **add** the **product** of -2 and -7. _____

8. If Laurie **saves** $20 per week, how much is this per year? _____

9. What **unit of measurement** might be used to compare amounts of trace elements in a food? _____

10. If n is a **whole number**, can $n - 1$ be **even**?   Yes   No

11. $^3/_5 + 0.4 =$ _____

12. Find the **volume** of this cake. $(V = \pi r^2 b)$ _____

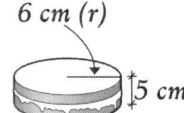
6 cm (r)
5 cm

13. **Twenty percent** is equal to _____ parts out of 100.

14. What **dimensions** are needed to box the cake in Question 12? _____

15. What type of graph is this? s_____

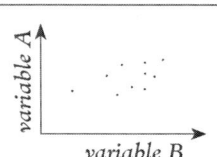
variable A
variable B

16. If the **average** of four scores is 49, what is the **total** of the scores? _____

17. Another term for the **intersection** of a network of **paths** is a j_____.

18. Which student is second tallest? _____

B   A
C   D
age
height

19. $2^3 =$ _____

20. $25 \div 0.01 =$ _____

Score: _____ /20 _____ %

Day 2

1. Evaluate 3^{-1}. _____

2. $0.7 + 0.06 =$ _____

3. $0.7 - 0.06 =$ _____

4. $0.7 \times 0.06 =$ _____

5. $0.7 \div 0.06$ (as a fraction) $=$ _____

6. Find the **perimeter** of this **triangle**. _____

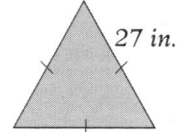
27 in.

7. To the **sum** of -11 and -6, **add** the **product** of -3 and -4. _____

8. If Leif saves $15 per week, how much is this per year? _____

9. What **unit of measurement** might be used to compare trace elements in vitamins? _____

10. If n is a **whole number**, can $2n + 1$ be **even**?   Yes   No

11. $^1/_5 + 0.8 =$ _____

12. The **perimeter** of a **circle** is called the _____.

13. **Twenty percent** is equal to _____ parts out of 1000.

14. The longest **chord** of a **circle** is the _____.

15. If Daniel **bought** mining company shares for $0.50 and **sold** them for $0.45, what percentage of the original price is his **loss**? _____

16. If the **average** of three scores is 49, what is the **total** of the scores? _____

17. $\pi = 3.1\overline{4}$ True   False

18. Which student is second youngest? _____

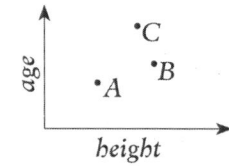
C
B
A
age
height

19. $\sqrt[3]{2^3} =$ _____

20. $25 \times 0.01 =$ _____

Score: _____ /20 _____ %

Day 3

1. Evaluate 4^{-1}. _____   2. $0.7 + 0.07 =$ _____

3. $0.7 - 0.07 =$ _____

4. $0.7 \times 0.07 =$ _____

5. $0.7 \div 0.07 =$ _____

6. Today's date in **international standard date** notation is _____YYYY__/__MM__/__DD__.

7. To the **sum** of −8 and −5, **add** the **product** of −2 and −6. _____

8. If Liam **saves** $10 per week, how much is this per year? _____

9. What **unit of measurement** is used to compare the **capacity** of swimming pools? _____

10. If n is a **whole number**, can $3n + 1$ be **even**?   Yes   No

11. $3^6 \div 3^2 =$ _____

12. A part smaller than half of the **circumference** of a **circle** is a

    _____.

13. **Thirty percent** is equal to _____ parts out of 100.

14. If Theo **bought** mining company shares for $0.20 and **sold** them for $0.28, what percentage of the original price is his **profit**? _____

15. What type of graph would be best to show **correlation** between **height** and **arm span**?

    _____

16. If the **average** of five scores is 49, what is the **total** of the scores? _____

17. $^{22}/_7 = \pi$ True   False

18. In a diving competition, Gabby received these **scores**: 8.1, 8.3, 8.0, 8.2, 7.9, 7.5, 7.7, 7.8. Ignoring the highest and lowest, what was her total score? _____

19. $0.01 \times 0.02 =$ _____

20. What is the **circumference** of a regulation-size basketball? _____

Score: _____ /20 _____ %

Day 4

1. Evaluate 5^{-1}. _____   2. $0.7 + 0.08 =$ _____

3. $0.7 - 0.08 =$ _____

4. $0.7 \times 0.08 =$ _____

5. $0.7 \div 0.08$ **simplified** is _____.

6. How much **annual simple interest** is earned on $2000 invested at 7.25% for three years?

    _____

7. To the **sum** of −9 and −6, **add** the **product** of −2 and −1. _____

8. If Lauren **saves** $25 per week, how much is this per year? _____

9. What **unit of mass** is used to measure luggage? _____

10. If n is a **whole number**, can $2n + 2$ be **even**?   Yes   No

11. $(3^2)^2 =$ _____

12. A larger part than half of the **circumference** of a **circle** is a

    _____.

13. **Thirty percent** is equal to _____ parts out of 1000.

14. If Tim **bought** mining company shares for $0.02 and **sold** them for $0.20, what percentage of the original price is his **profit**? _____

15. The point (0, 0) where the x-axis and the y-axis meet in the coordinate plane is called the

    _____.

16. If the **average** of six scores is 49, what is the **total** of the scores? _____

17. $1000 \div 0.5 =$ _____

18. In a gymnastics competition, Gail received these **scores**: 5.1, 5.3, 6.0, 6.2, 5.9, 5.5, 5.7, 5.9. Ignoring the highest and lowest, what was her total score? _____

19. $0.01 \times 0.03 =$ _____

20. How many **quadrants** are there in a Cartesian plane? _____

Score: _____ /20 _____ %

Week 8

Day 1

1. Evaluate 10^{-2}. _____

2. $0.7 + 0.09 =$ _____

3. $0.7 - 0.09 =$ _____

4. $0.7 \times 0.09 =$ _____

5. $0.7 \div 0.09$ (as a fraction) = _____

6. $2^3 \div 2^3 =$ _____

7. From the **sum** of –6 and –5, **subtract** the **product** of –2 and –1.

   _____

8. If Lincoln **saves** $60 per week, how much is this per year?

   _____

9. What **unit of measurement** is used to compare the **capacities** of reservoirs?

   _____

10. If n is a **whole number**, can $2n$ be **even**?   Yes   No

11. $2^3 =$ _____

12. $0.01 \times 0.4 =$ _____

13. What **percentage** of 50 is 25? _____

14. If Charlie **bought** mining company shares for $0.10 and **sold** them for $0.25, what percentage of the original price is his **profit**?

    _____

15. When it is easy to judge an amount without having to count, we e_____.

16. If the **average** of six scores is 47, what is the **total** of the scores?

    _____

17. What **fraction** of a **kilometer** is a **meter**? _____

18. How many of something is a **baker's dozen**?

    _____

19. $100 \div 0.05 =$ _____

20. Can 10 be a **prime factor** of 70?   Yes   No

Day 2

1. $\sqrt{1/4} \times \sqrt{1/4} =$ _____

2. $0.8 + 0.01 =$ _____

3. $0.8 - 0.01 =$ _____

4. $0.8 \times 0.01 =$ _____

5. $0.8 \div 0.01 =$ _____

6. $3^3 \div 3^3 =$ _____

7. From the **sum** of –3 and –2, **subtract** the **product** of –2 and –1. _____

8. If Franklin **saves** $75 per week, how much is this per year? _____

9. What **unit of measurement** is usually used for liquid medicines? _____

10. If n is a **whole number**, can $n - 2$ be **even**?   Yes   No

11. $2^4 =$ _____

12. $0.01 \times 0.05 =$ _____

13. What **percentage** of 80 is 20? _____

14. If Tai **bought** mining company shares for $2.50 and **sold** them for $10.00, what percentage of the original price is his **profit**?

    _____

15. The measures of two **supplementary angles** must total

    _____.

16. If the **average** of seven scores is 46, what is the **total** of the scores? _____

17. Can a **square pyramid** be a **platonic solid**?

    Yes   No

18. If life expectancy was once **three score years and ten**, what age is that? _____

19. $100 \div 0.01 =$ _____

20. What percentage of students would be in the top **quartile**? _____

Score: _____ /20   %   Score: _____ /20   %

Day 3

1. **Evaluate** 7^{-2}. _____

2. $0.9 + 0.9 =$ _____

3. $0.98 - 0.9 =$ _____

4. $0.01 \times 0.06 =$ _____

5. $1600 \div 0.4 =$ _____

6. $26^0 =$ _____

7. From the **sum** of -2 and -1, **subtract** the **product** of -2 and -1. _____

8. If Ferdie **saves** $70 per week, how much is this per year? _____

9. Which **unit of measurement** is commonly used to compare the **weights** of suitcases?

   _____

10. What number other than four can be the **square root** of 16? _____

11. **Bivariate** data means there are _____.

12. A **translation** is also called a

    _____

13. What **percentage** of 60 is 15? _____

14. $80 \div 4 =$ _____

15. What **fraction** of one dollar is one cent? _____

16. If the **average** of four scores is 24, what is the **total** of the scores?

    _____

17. The **product** of any number and one is always

    _____.

18. Express the **prime factors** of 64 in **exponent form**.

    _____

19. What is a **ray**? _____

    _____

20. What **percentage** of students would be in the lowest quartile? _____

Day 4

1. **Evaluate** $\sqrt{1/3} \times \sqrt{1/3}$. _____

2. $0.9 + 0.89 =$ _____

3. $0.9 - 0.89 =$ _____

4. $0.01 \times 0.07 =$ _____

5. $2500 \div 0.5 =$ _____

6. $13^0 =$ _____

7. From the **sum** of -4 and -3, **subtract** the **product** of -2 and -1. _____

8. If José **saves** $90 per week, how much is this per year? _____

9. Which **unit of measurement** is commonly used to measure a person's **weight**?

   _____

10. What is the **cube root** of -27? _____

11. A line that intersects a **circle** at a single point perpendicular to the **radius** is a _____.

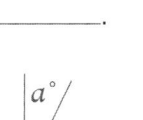

12. The measures of two **complementary angles** sum to _____.

13. What **percentage** of 75 is 15? _____

14. $100 \div 0.1 =$ _____

15. What **fraction** of a dollar is 20 cents? _____

16. If the **average** of three scores is 24, what is the **total** of the scores? _____

17. Any number to the **power of one** is

    _____.

18. Express the **prime factors** of 56 in **exponent form**.

    _____

19. A **cross section** of a **cone** produces what **shape**?

    _____

20. An **inverse equation** for $120 \times 4 = x$ is

    _____.

Score: /20   %   Score: /20   %

Week 9

Day 1

1. Evaluate 8^{-2}. _____

2. $0.01 + 0.08 =$ _____

3. $0.01 - 0.08 =$ _____

4. $0.01 \times 0.08 =$ _____

5. $1600 \div 0.04 =$ _____

6. $(12a^2b^3)^0 =$ _____

7. During a 35%-off book sale, how much would an $18 book **cost**? _____

8. If Tabitha **saves** $14 per week, how much is this per year? _____

9. What **unit of measurement** might be used to measure parts of a cell? _____

10. **Round** 0.331 to one **significant digit**. _____

11. What is the **value** of c on this **number line**?

    0   12 c 36

    _____

12. An **inverse equation** for $4 \times 5 = 20$ is

    _____.

13. What **percentage** is 15 of 90? _____

14. If Julia **bought** mining company shares for $0.25 and **sold** them for $0.275, what percentage of the original price is her **profit**? _____

15. How many **common members** are in two **disjoint** sets? _____

16. If the **average** of five scores is 20, what is the **total** of the scores? _____

17. $5^1 =$ _____

18. Express 1990 in **Roman numerals**.

    _____

19. Find the value of $x°$.

    _____ $89°$ $x°$

20. What **fraction** of a **kilometer** is a **centimeter**?

    _____

Score: _____ /20   _____ %

Day 2

1. Evaluate $\sqrt{1/2} \times \sqrt{1/2}$. _____

2. $0.01 + 0.09 =$ _____   3. $0.01 - 0.09 =$ _____

4. $0.01 \times 0.09 =$ _____

5. $3.2 \div 0.8 =$ _____

6. $2^0 =$ _____

7. During a 35%-off book sale, how much would a $20 book **cost**? _____

8. If Talia **saves** $16 per week, how much is this per year? _____

9. What **unit of measurement** might be used to measure the **length** of a mosquito? _____

10. **Round** 1.331 to one **significant digit**? _____

11. What is the **value** of d on this **number line**?

    -10 d -5 0   5

    _____

12. An **inverse equation** for $5 + 9 = 14$ is

    _____.

13. What **percentage** of 105 is 15? *(Answer to one decimal place.)* _____

14. If Damon **bought** mining company shares for $0.50 and **sold** them for $0.60, what percentage of the original price is his **profit**? _____

15. **Area** is the word used to describe the

    s_____ enclosed within a

    b_____.

16. If the **average** of four scores is 25, what is the **total** of the scores? _____

17. $6^0 =$ _____

18. Express 1999 in **Roman numerals**.

    _____

19. Find the value of $x°$.

    _____ $x°$ $23°$

20. What **fraction** of a **centimeter** is a **millimeter**? _____

Score: _____ /20   _____ %

Day 3

1. Evaluate 9^{-1}. _____
2. $0.01 + 0.1 =$ _____
3. $10 - 0.2 =$ _____
4. $0.01 \times 0.1 =$ _____
5. $12a^2b^0 =$ _____
6. $1000 \div 0.002 =$ _____
7. **Convert** $12\frac{1}{2}\%$ to a **fraction**. _____
8. If Georgia **saves** $100 per week, how much is this per year? _____
9. $\frac{3}{4} \times$ _____ $= 30$
10. What is the **value** of d on this **number line**?

    d -0.4 0

    _____

11. A box holds six cans in two rows of three. Each can is 11 cm **tall** and has a **radius** of 4 cm. What are the **dimensions** of the box? _____
12. A portion of a **circle** that is more than half and bound by an **arc** and two **radii** is a

    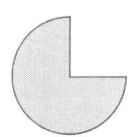

    _____ .
13. What **percentage** of 120 is 15? _____
14. If Habib **bought** shares in a company for $2 and **sold** them for $2.80, what percentage of the original price is his **profit**? _____
15. To **increase** or **decrease** the **size** of a figure is to d_____ its size.
16. If the **average** of four scores is 23, what is the **total** of the scores? _____
17. **Round** 482 to two **significant digits**. _____
18. Draw a **ray**.

19. Express 1910 in **Roman numerals**. _____
20. Another term for **boundary** is p_____ .

Day 4

1. Evaluate 8^{-1}. _____
2. $0.02 + 0.2 =$ _____
3. $10 - 0.28 =$ _____
4. $0.02 \times 0.02 =$ _____
5. $p^0 =$ _____
6. $1000 \div 0.005 =$ _____
7. **Convert** 15% to a **fraction**. _____
8. If Puneet and Meher **save** $200 per week, how much is this per year? _____
9. $\frac{3}{4} \times$ _____ $= 75$
10. What is the **value** of f on this **number line**?

    -1.5 0 f

    _____

11. A box holds six cans in two rows of three. Each can is 9 cm **tall** and has a **radius** of 3 cm. What are the **dimensions** of the box? _____
12. A portion of a **circle** that is less than half and bound by an **arc** and two **radii** is a

    _____
13. What **percentage** of 135 is 15? _____
14. If Roberto **bought** shares in a company for $2 and **sold** them for $3, what percentage of the original price is his **profit**? _____
15. An **inverse** **equation** for $20 - 6 = x$ is _____ .
16. If the **average** of five scores is 23, what is the **total** of the scores? _____
17. **Round** 331 to two **significant digits**. _____
18. Draw an **arc**.

19. Express 1992 in **Roman numerals**. _____
20. The relationship between a drawing's dimensions and the actual dimensions is called its

    _____ .

Score: _____ /20 _____ %

Score: _____ /20 _____ %

Week 10

Day 1	Day 2

Day 1

1. Evaluate 10^{-1}. _____

2. 14.16 + 19.63 = _____ 3. $3\frac{1}{3} - 1\frac{2}{3}$ = _____

4. 0.02 × 0.03 = _____ 5. 20 ÷ 0.04 = _____

6. $(3xp)^0$ = _____

7. Today's date in **international standard date** notation is __YYYY__ / __MM__ / __DD__ .

8. If Rahnee and Raj **save** $150 per week, how much is this per year? _____

9. $\frac{3}{4}$ × _____ = 37.5

10. Find the **perimeter** of this **isosceles triangle**.

   _____

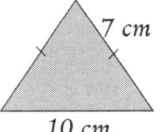
7 cm
10 cm

11. What is the **value** of g on this **number line**?

0   1000   g

   _____

12. Another term for **Cartesian coordinates** is

   o_____ p_____.

13. What **percentage** of 150 is 25? *(Answer to two decimal places.)* _____

14. Any **line segment** joining two points on a **circle** is a

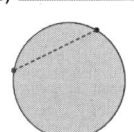

   _____.

15. How much will Sheena pay for a $20 meal if she uses her 15% discount card? _____

16. If the **average** of four scores is 82, what is the **total** of the scores? _____

17. Express 1890 in **Roman numerals**.

   _____

18. Draw a **chord**.

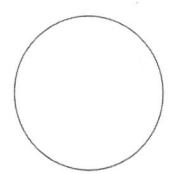

19. **Round** 567 to one **significant digit**. _____

20. 20 ÷ 0.001 = _____

Day 2

1. Evaluate $4^7/4^3$. _____

2. 49.75 + 25.25 = _____

3. $3 - \frac{2}{7}$ = _____

4. 0.02 × 0.04 = _____

5. 20 ÷ 0.05 = _____

6. $3x^0$ = _____

7. In a 35%-reduced book sale, how much would a $10 book **cost**? _____

8. If Raina **saves** $140 per week, how much is this per year? _____

9. $\frac{3}{4}$ × _____ = 45

10. Find the **perimeter** of this **isosceles triangle**.

   _____

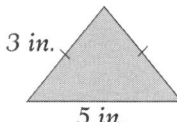
3 in.
5 in.

11. What is the **value** of b on this **number line**?

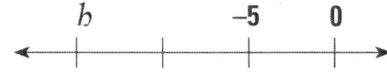
b   −5   0

   _____

12. A solid in which all angles and faces are congruent is called a _____ solid.

13. What **percentage** of 250 is 25? _____

14. Which type of **prism** is not a **polyhedron**?

   _____

15. How much will Sheba pay for her $15 meal if she uses her 15% discount card? _____

16. If the **average** of five scores is 82, what is the **total** of the scores? _____

17. Express 1994 in **Roman numerals**.

   _____

18. Draw a **tangent**.

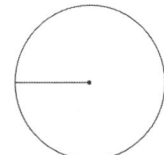

19. **Round** 31 to one **significant digit**. _____

20. 700 × 0.0002 = _____

Score:	/20	%	Score:	/20	%

Day 3

1. Evaluate 10^{-1}. _____

2. $20 + 0.05 =$ _____

3. $20 - 0.05 =$ _____

4. $20 \times 0.05 =$ _____

5. $20 \div 0.05 =$ _____

6. $7t^0 =$ _____

7. Are the two **diagonals** of any **parallelogram** equal in length?   Yes   No

8. If Lucas **saves** $120 per week, how much is this per year? _____

9. $^3/_4 \times$ _____ $= 60$

10. Using $a^2 + b^2 = c^2$, find the length of the **hypotenuse** of this **triangle**.

    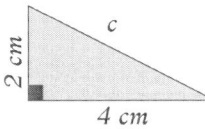

    _____

11. What is the **value** of i on this **number line**?

    _____

12. Estimate the **area** of your school gymnasium.

    _____

13. What **percentage** of 500 is 25? _____

14. Crystals that form **prisms** with bases that are not aligned directly above each other are called

    o_____ prisms.

15. How much will Sydney pay for a $25 meal if she uses her 15% discount card?

    _____

16. **Convert** 4500 mm into **meters**. _____

17. **Round** 3.67 to two **significant digits**. _____

18. Express 1995 in **Roman numerals**.

    _____

19. **Simplify** $3m^3 \times 5m$. _____

20. $1.2 \div 0.003 =$ _____

Day 4

1. If $9^m = {}^1/_{81}$, find the **value** of m. _____

2. $200 + 0.01 =$ _____

3. $200 - 0.01 =$ _____

4. $200 \times 0.01 =$ _____

5. $200 \div 0.01 =$ _____

6. $12w^0 \div 4c^0 =$ _____

7. Find the **value** of $x°$.

    _____

    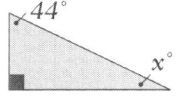

8. If Luke and Leila save $800 per week, how much is this per year?

    _____

9. $^3/_4 \times$ _____ $= 90$

10. Using $a^2 + b^2 = c^2$, find the length of the **hypotenuse** of this **triangle**.

    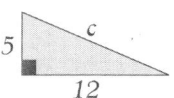

    _____

11. What is the **value** of j on this **number line**?

    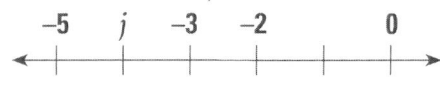

    _____

12. **Estimate** the **perimeter** of your school gymnasium.

    _____

13. What **percentage** of 200 is 25? _____

14. How many **radii** are there in a **diameter**?

    _____

15. How much will Sid pay for a $20 book if he uses his 15% discount card?

    _____

16. **Convert** 750 mL into **liters**. _____

17. **Round** 0.331 to two **significant digits**. _____

18. Express 1997 in **Roman numerals**.

    _____

19. **Simplify** $6m^2 \times 3m^2$. _____

20. $1.2 \div 0.004 =$ _____

Day 1

1. Evaluate 2^{-2}. _____
2. $30 + 0.05 =$ _____
3. $30 - 0.05 =$ _____
4. $30 \times 0.05 =$ _____
5. $30 \div 0.05 =$ _____
6. $24g^3 \div 6g^3 =$ _____
7. Draw **perpendicular lines**.

8. If Henri **saves** $95 per week, how much is this per year? _____
9. $^1/_4 \times$ _____ $= 60$
10. **Calculate** the **sum** of the **whole numbers** from one to one hundred. _____
11. If Natalia's **average** after three tests is 80%, what must she score on her next test to raise her average to 84%? _____
12. What is the **temperature** of boiling water? _____
13. What **percentage** of 2000 is 25? _____
14. A **radius** is what fraction of the **diameter**? _____
15. What **time** is it in Philadelphia if it is 6:00 a.m. in Flagstaff and Philadelphia is two hours ahead? _____
16. What are the **dimensions** of a box that holds six cans in rows of three and each can is 10 cm **tall** and has a **radius** of 3 cm? _____
17. **Round** 2331 to one **significant digit**. _____
18. Express 1998 in **Roman numerals**. _____
19. $40 \times 0.6 =$ _____   20. $\sqrt{4^2} + 3^2 =$ _____

Day 2

1. If $2^z = 0.25$, find the **value** of z. _____
2. $20 + 0.04 =$ _____
3. $20 - 0.04 =$ _____
4. $20 \times 0.04 =$ _____
5. $20 \div 0.04 =$ _____
6. $2a^0 + 4c^0 =$ _____
7. What is the **size** of the **angle** at which **perpendicular lines** meet? _____
8. If Bonnie and Clyde **save** $300 per week, how much is this per year? _____
9. $^1/_4 \times$ _____ $= 50$
10. **Calculate** the **sum** of the **whole numbers** from one to one thousand. _____
11. If Bryce's **average** after three tests is 81%, what must he score on his next test to raise his average to 82%? _____
12. What **instrument** might be used to measure the **temperature** of water? _____
13. What **percentage** of 1500 is 15? _____
14. The **ratio** of the **diameter** to the **radius** is _____.
15. If it is 6:00 a.m. in Atlanta, what **time** is it in Eugene, Oregon if Atlanta is three hours ahead? _____
16. If Bob scored $^{28}/_{30}$ on a math test and $^{48}/_{50}$ on a science test, which was his better score?
    (a) $^{28}/_{30}$ (b) $^{48}/_{50}$
17. **Round** 3314 to one **significant digit**. _____
18. Express 1550 in **Roman numerals**. _____
19. What is the **length** of a football field? _____
20. The **quotient** of eighteen and six is _____.

Day 3

1. Evaluate 10^{-3}. _____

2. $0.03 + 0.003 =$ _____

3. $0.03 - 0.003 =$ _____

4. $0.03 \times 0.003 =$ _____

5. $0.03 \div 0.003 =$ _____

6. $3d^0 + 6e^0 =$ _____

7. $(+3) + (-18) =$ _____

8. If Lorrae **saves** $200 per week, how much is this per year?

   _____

9. $\frac{1}{4} \times$ _____ $= 30$

10. $6 + (9 - 2) \times 4 =$ _____

11. Write an inequality for the **value** of k on this **number line**.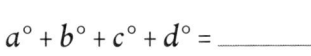

    _____

12. How many **permutations** are there for **ordering** the letters A, B, and C?

    _____

13. Complete the **equation** for the angle sum of this **cyclic quadrilateral**.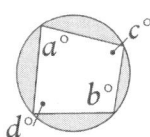

    $a° + b° + c° + d° =$ _____

14. **Expand** $(y + x)^2$. _____

15. One out of four as a **percentage** is _____.

16. If Gil scored $\frac{38}{40}$ on a math test, $\frac{49}{50}$ on an English test, and $\frac{78}{80}$ on a science test, which was his best score?

    (a) $\frac{38}{40}$ (b) $\frac{49}{50}$ (c) $\frac{78}{80}$

17. **Round** 2486 to two **significant digits**. _____

18. Express 1993 in **Roman numerals**.

    _____

19. $100 \div 0.002 =$ _____

20. How many **dozen** are there in 144? _____

Score: /20   %

Day 4

1. If $2^x = \frac{1}{8}$, then x is _____.

2. $0.002 + 0.0020 =$ _____

3. $0.002 - 0.002 =$ _____

4. $0.002 \times 0.002 =$ _____

5. $0.002 \div 0.002 =$ _____

6. $10z^0 + 4y^0 =$ _____

7. $(+18) \times (-3) =$ _____

8. If Colin and Rose together **save** $250 per week, how much is this per year?

   _____

9. $\frac{1}{4} \times$ _____ $= 40$

10. $27 - (4 \times 2) + 9 =$ _____

11. Write an inequality for the **value** of l on this **number line**.

    _____

12. How many **permutations** are there for **ordering** the letters X, Y, and Z?

    _____

13. One **angle** of a **triangle** in a **semicircle** is a

    _____ angle.

14. **Expand** $(y + 2)^2$. _____

15. Three out of five as a **percentage** is _____.

16. If Bo scored $\frac{28}{40}$ on a math test and $\frac{48}{60}$ on a science test, which was his better score?

    (a) $\frac{28}{40}$ (b) $\frac{48}{60}$

17. **Round** 3315 to three **significant digits**. _____

18. Express 1919 in **Roman numerals**.

    _____

19. $0.05 \div 0.005 =$ _____

20. The **product** of eighteen and three is _____.

Score: /20   %

Day 1

1. Evaluate 10^{-2}. _____

2. $0.04 + 0.004 =$ _____

3. $0.04 - 0.004 =$ _____

4. $0.04 \times 0.004 =$ _____

5. $0.04 \div 0.004 =$ _____

6. Simplify $(5^2)^3$. _____

7. $(-10) \times (-4) =$ _____

8. If Darcy and Ella **save** $400 per week, how much is this per year?

   _____

9. $^1/_4 \times$ _____ $= 160$

10. Complete the **pattern**. 3, 9, 27, _____, _____

11. What is the **value** of m on this **number line**?

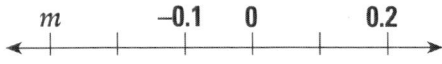

   _____

12. Use **tally marks** to show 15.

   _____

13. A **pentagonal pyramid** has _____ vertices.

14. $(x + 7)^2 =$ _____

15. Calculate the **area** of this **parallelogram** if $A = bh$.

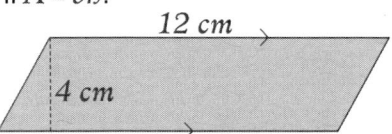

   _____

16. If Chris scored $^{25}/_{30}$ on a math test and $^{40}/_{50}$ on a science test, which was his better score?

   (a) $^{25}/_{30}$ (b) $^{40}/_{50}$

17. **Twenty-five percent** is the same as one out of _____.

18. Express 1991 in **Roman numerals**.

   _____

19. Express 0.0334 in **scientific notation**.

   _____

20. How many **dozen** are there in 288? _____

Score: _____ /20   _____ %

Day 2

1. If 2^g is $^1/_{16}$, then $g =$ _____

2. $100 + 0.02 =$ _____

3. $100 - 0.02 =$ _____

4. $100 \times 0.02 =$ _____

5. $100 \div 0.02 =$ _____

6. Simplify $(5^3)^3$. _____

7. $(-2) \times (3) =$ _____

8. If Lauren **spends** $15 per week, how much is this per year?

   _____

9. $^1/_4 \times$ _____ $= 360$

10. Complete the **pattern**. 2, 4, 8, _____, _____, _____

11. What is the **value** of n on this **number line**?

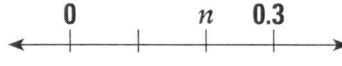

   _____

12. Use **tally marks** to show 25. _____

13. What type of **pyramid** is not a **polyhedron**?

   _____

14. $(a - 9)^2 =$ _____

15. Calculate the **area** of this **parallelogram** if $A = bh$.

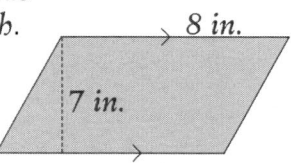

   _____

16. If Sarah scored $^{22}/_{30}$ on a math test and $^{42}/_{50}$ on a science test, which was her better score?

   (a) $^{22}/_{30}$ (b) $^{42}/_{50}$

17. **Two hundred and fifty percent** is the same as 25 out of _____.

18. Express 1981 in **Roman numerals**.

   _____

19. **Round** 0.361 to one **significant digit**.

   _____

20. How many **dozen** are there in 432? _____

Score: _____ /20   _____ %

Day 3

1. **Evaluate** 10^{-3}. _____

2. $0.06 + 0.006 =$ _____

3. $0.06 - 0.006 =$ _____

4. $0.06 \times 0.006 =$ _____

5. $0.06 \div 0.006 =$ _____

6. $^1/_4$ as a **percentage** is _____ .

7. During a 35%-off book sale, how much would a $19 book **cost**?

   _____

8. If a class of 30 students has five absentees, what **fraction** of the class is not there?

   _____

9. $^1/_4 \times$ _____ $= 0.60$

10. If Annie **saves** $240 per week, how much is this per year?

    _____

11. What is the **value** of o on this **number line**?

    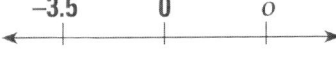

    _____

12. $(+11) + (-9) =$ _____

13. Which 3-D **shape** is made of 12 **regular pentagon** faces?

    _____

14. $(m - 2)^2 =$ _____

15. **PEMDAS** is a **mnemonic** for the o_____ of

    o_____ .

16. **Forty-five percent** is the same as nine out of _____ .

17. Express 63,200 in **scientific notation**.

    _____

18. Express 1900 in **Roman numerals**.

    _____

19. $100 \div 0.5 =$ _____

20. How many **dozen** are there in 492? _____

Day 4

1. If $2^t = {}^1/_{32}$, then $t =$ _____

2. $0.07 + 0.007 =$ _____

3. $0.07 - 0.007 =$ _____

4. $0.07 \times 0.007 =$ _____

5. $0.07 \div 0.007 =$ _____

6. $^1/_8$ as a **percentage** is _____ .

7. During a 35%-off book sale, how much would an $11 book **cost**?

   _____

8. If 8 students out of a class of 32 are away at a sports event, what **fraction** of the class is left?

   _____

9. $^1/_4 \times$ _____ $= 1$

10. If Francesca **saves** $40 per week, how much is this per year?

    _____

11. What is the **value** of p on this **number line**?

    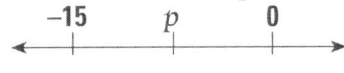

    _____

12. $(-3) + (-8) =$ _____

13. Which 3-D **shape** is made of 20 **equilateral triangular** faces? _____

14. $(y - 5)^2 =$ _____

15. Draw a **tangent**.

    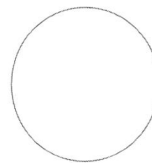

16. **Fifty percent** is the same as one out of _____ .

17. Express 0.00186 in **scientific notation**.

    _____

18. Express 1905 in **Roman numerals**.

    _____

19. $100 \div 0.05 =$ _____

20. How many **dozen** are there in 576? _____

Score:	/20	%

Week 13

Day 1

1. Evaluate 10^{-2}. _____

2. $0.08 + 0.008 =$ _____

3. $0.08 - 0.008 =$ _____

4. $0.08 \times 0.008 =$ _____

5. $0.08 \div 0.008 =$ _____

6. $^2/_3$ as a **decimal** is _____.

7. During a 35%-off book sale, how much would a $12 book **cost**?

   _____

8. Write **two hundred and fifty billion** in numerical form.

   _____

9. $^1/_4 \times$ _____ $= 20$

10. If Frances **saves** $140 per week, how much is this per year?

    _____

11. What is the **value** of q on this **number line**?

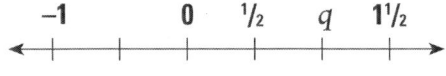

    _____

12. Find the **reciprocal** of 1. _____

13. Eight joined **regular equilateral triangular** faces make what 3-D **shape**?

    _____

14. $(2a + 1)^2 =$ _____

15. $3 < 7$ is called an i_____.

16. This 2-D figure is called an

    o_____ c_____.

17. Express 0.472×100 in **scientific notation**.

    _____

18. Express 1984 in **Roman numerals**.

    _____

19. $10 \div 0.01 =$ _____

20. How many **dozen** are there in 720?

    _____

Day 2

1. If $9^e = {}^1/_{81}$, then $e =$ _____

2. $0.09 + 0.009 =$ _____

3. $0.09 - 0.009 =$ _____

4. $0.09 \times 0.009 =$ _____

5. $0.09 \div 0.009 =$ _____

6. $^1/_5$ as a **percentage** is _____.

7. During a 35%-off book sale, how much would a $25 book **cost**? _____

8. Write 25 in **scientific notation**.

   _____

9. $^1/_4 \times$ _____ $= 25$

10. If Helen Rose **saves** $65 per week, how much is this per year?

    _____

11. What is the **value** of r on this **number line**?

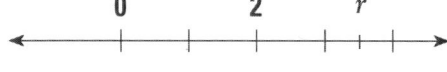

    _____

12. Find the **reciprocal** of 0.1. _____

13. Four joined **regular equilateral triangular** faces make what 3-D **shape**?

    _____.

14. $(3y - 1)^2 =$ _____

15. This 2D figure is a simple

    _____ _____.

16. What method might be used to weigh a whale?

    _____

    _____

17. Express 0.0631×10 in **scientific notation**.

    _____

18. Express 1954 in **Roman numerals**.

    _____

19. $10 \div 0.02 =$ _____

20. How many **dozen** are there in 864? _____

Score: _____ /20 _____ %

Score: _____ /20 _____ %

Day 3

1. Evaluate 4^{-3}. _____

2. $10 + 0.5 =$ _____

3. $10 - 0.5 =$ _____

4. $10 \times 0.5 =$ _____

5. $10 \div 0.5 =$ _____

6. $^5/_6$ as a **decimal** is _____.

7. **Simplify** s^8/s^4. _____

8. Write 690 in **scientific notation**.

   _____

9. $^1/_4 \times$ _____ $= 12$

10. If Thomas **saves** $80 per week, how much is this per year?

    _____

11. What is the **value** of s on this **number line**?

    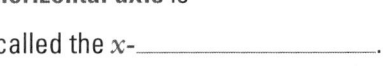

    _____

12. Find the **reciprocal** of 0.2. _____

13. What 3-D **shape** does six joined **regular congruent square** faces make?

    _____

14. $(5a - 1)^2 =$ _____

15. How might you calculate the mass of a dolphin?

    d_____

16. Express 1920 in **scientific notation**.

    _____

17. In an election, Peter Pacton received 40% of the vote while Betty Wayne received 45%. If Pacton received 52,000 votes, how many did Wayne receive?

    _____

18. Express 1959 in **Roman numerals**.

    _____

19. $100 \times 0.001 =$ _____

20. How many **dozen** are there in 1008? _____

Day 4

1. Evaluate $\sqrt{4} + \sqrt{9}$. _____

2. $10 + 0.005 =$ _____

3. $10 - 0.005 =$ _____

4. $10 \times 0.005 =$ _____

5. $10 \div 0.005 =$ _____

6. $^1/_3$ as a **decimal** is _____.

7. Evaluate $2^8/2^4$. _____

8. 990 in **scientific notation** is _____.

9. $^1/_4 \times$ _____ $= 6$

10. If Antonio **saves** $240 per week, how much is this per year?

    _____

11. What is the **value** of t on this **number line**?

    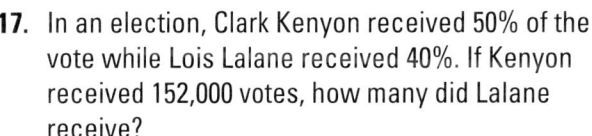

    _____

12. Find the **reciprocal** of 0.3. _____

13. How many **edges** are there on a **cylinder**?

    _____

14. $(4a + 1)^2 =$ _____

15. The **point** at which a path crosses the **horizontal axis** is

    called the x-_____.

16. Express 2009 in **scientific notation**.

    _____

17. In an election, Clark Kenyon received 50% of the vote while Lois Lalane received 40%. If Kenyon received 152,000 votes, how many did Lalane receive?

    _____

18. Express 1955 in **Roman numerals**.

    _____

19. $1000 \times 0.001 =$ _____

20. How many **dozen** are there in 1152?

    _____

Score: /20 %

Score: /20 %

Week 14

Day 1

1. Evaluate 5^{-2}. _____

2. $5 + 0.05 =$ _____

3. $5 - 0.05 =$ _____

4. $5 \times 0.05 =$ _____

5. $5 \div 0.05 =$ _____

6. $^4/_5$ as a **decimal** is _____.

7. Today's date in **international standard date** notation is _YYYY_/_MM_/_DD_.

8. 0.0689 in **scientific notation** is

   _____.

9. $^1/_4 \times$ _____ $= 30$

10. Express 1996 in **scientific notation**.

    _____

11. What is the **value** of u on this **number line**?

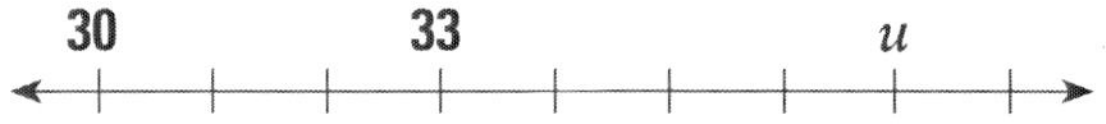

    30   33 u
    ◄─┼─┼─┼─┼─┼─┼─┼─┼─┼─►

    _____

12. Find the **reciprocal** of 0.4. _____

13. How many **edges** does a **sphere** have?

    _____

14. If 1.2 billion people live in China, express this as a **ratio** of the world's population of six billion.

    _____

15. A box holds six cans in rows of two. Each can is 12 cm **tall** and has a **radius** of 4 cm. What are

    the **dimensions** of the box? _____

16. Five cents **fewer** than $5 is _____.

17. In a class election, Bartholomew received 30% of the votes while Lisa received 40%. If 15 students voted for Bartholomew, how many voted for Lisa?

    _____

18. Express 1952 in **Roman numerals**.

    _____

19. $200 \times 0.002 =$ _____

20. How many **dozen** are there in 1296? _____

Day 2

1. Evaluate 3^{-2}. _____

2. $10 + 0.05 =$ _____

3. $10 - 0.05 =$ _____

4. $10 \times 0.05 =$ _____

5. $10 \div 0.05 =$ _____

6. $^1/_6$ as a **decimal** is _____.

7. During a 35%-off book sale, how much would a $7 book cost?

   _____

8. 0.0012 in **scientific notation** is

   _____.

9. $^1/_4 \times$ _____ $= 15$

10. Express 1997 in **scientific notation**.

    _____

11. What is the **value** of v on this **number line**?

    _____

    (number line with marks, 1 at top, 0 below, v at bottom)

12. Find the **reciprocal** of 0.5.

    _____

13. How many **faces** does a **sphere** have? _____

14. If 21 million people live in Australia, express this as a **ratio** of the world's population of six billion.

    _____

15. The point at which a **path** crosses the **vertical axis** is

    called the y-i_____.

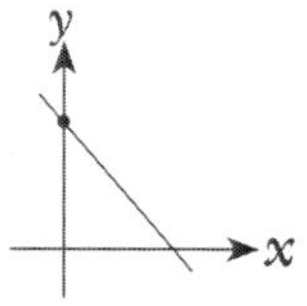

    (graph with x and y axes, downward sloping line)

16. Five cents **fewer** than $10 is _____.

17. In an election, Peter received 45% of the vote while Bruce received 44%. If 45,000 voted for

    Peter, how many voted for Bruce? _____

18. Express 1958 in **Roman numerals**.

    _____

19. $200 \times 0.003 =$ _____

20. How many **dozen** are there in 1308? _____

Score: _____ /20   %

Score: _____ /20   %

Day 3

1. Evaluate 6^{-2}. _____

2. $3 + 0.05 =$ _____
3. $3 - 0.05 =$ _____

4. $3 \times 0.05 =$ _____
5. $3 \div 0.05 =$ _____

6. $^1/_{10,000}$ as a **decimal** is _____.

7. Is this network **traversable**?

    Yes   No

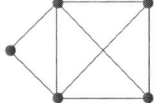

8. $2.4 \times 10^6 =$ _____

9. $^1/_4 \times$ _____ $= 14$

10. The symbol **AU** stands for

    a_____ u_____.

11. As a **percentage** of the whole, what is the **value** of w?

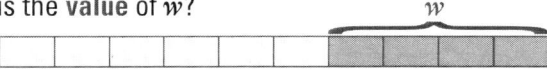

    _____

12. List the pairs of **opposite** angles.

    _____

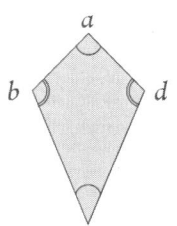

13. How many **edges** are there on a **square pyramid**?

    _____

14. A number that is the square of an integer is called a p_____ s_____.

15. If Byron's **average** after three tests is 77%, what must he score on his next test to make his average 80%? _____

16. If a **circle** is divided into 12 equal **sectors**, what is the angle measure of each **segment**?

    _____

17. Is this network **traversable**?

    Yes   No

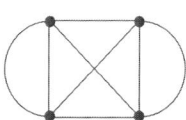

18. Express 0.0334 in **scientific notation**.

    _____

19. $200 \times 0.004 =$ _____

20. How many **dozen** are there in 1320? _____

Day 4

1. Evaluate 4^{-2}. _____

2. $4 + 0.05 =$ _____

3. $4 - 0.05 =$ _____

4. $4 \times 0.05 =$ _____

5. $4 \div 0.05 =$ _____

6. $^{89}/_{100}$ as a **decimal** is _____.

7. Is this network **traversable**?

    Yes   No

8. 99% of 300 = _____

9. $^1/_4 \times$ _____ $= 17$

10. What **distance** is one **astronomical unit**?

    _____

    _____

11. As a **percentage** of the whole, what is the **value** of x?

    _____

12. The word **velocity** refers to s_____ in a particular d_____.

13. The **symbol** for **velocity** is _____.

14. **Vehicle speed** is commonly **measured** in _____.

15. What is an **intercept**? _____

    _____

16. If a **circle** is divided into 24 equal **sectors**, what is the angle measure of each **segment**?

    _____

17. Is this network **traversable**?

    Yes   No

18. Express 0.08674 in **scientific notation**.

    _____

19. $200 \times 0.005 =$ _____

20. How many **dozen** are there in 1332? _____

Score: /20   %

Score: /20   %

Day 1

1. Evaluate 7^{-2}. _____

2. $1.5 + 0.05 =$ _____ 3. $1.5 - 0.05 =$ _____

4. $1.5 \times 0.05 =$ _____

5. $1.5 \div 0.05 =$ _____

6. $^1/_{100}$ as a **decimal** is _____.

7. Is this network **traversable**?

   Yes   No

8. An example of **exponential growth** is

   _____.

9. $^1/_4 \times$ _____ $= 18$

10. Name a **fraction** that is an example of a **recurring decimal**. _____

11. If Beau's **average** after three tests is 63%, what must he score on his next test to make his average 65%? _____

12. Find the **reciprocal** of 0.6. _____

13. The term **asymmetry** refers to something having

    _____

    _____.

14. What type of **transformation** is this?

    _____

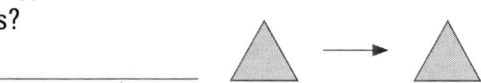

15. Any number that cannot be expressed as a **fraction** is an i_____ number.

16. If a **circle** is divided into six equal **sectors**, what is the angle measure of each **segment**? _____

17. Express 0.1334 in **scientific notation**.

    _____

18. Express 1956 in **Roman numerals**.

    _____

19. $200 \times 0.006 =$ _____

20. Write an example of an **irrational** number.

    _____

Score: _____ /20 _____ %

Day 2

1. Evaluate 2^{-2}. _____

2. $2 + 0.05 =$ _____

3. $2 - 0.05 =$ _____

4. $2 \times 0.05 =$ _____

5. $2 \div 0.05 =$ _____

6. $^1/_{1000}$ as a **decimal** is _____.

7. Is this network **traversable**?

   Yes   No

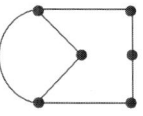

8. If a **circle** is cut into 20 equal **sectors**, what is the angle measure of each **segment**?

   _____

9. $^1/_4 \times$ _____ $= 19$

10. A **half-line** is also known as a _____.

11. What type of **equation** is $x + y = 5$?

    _____

12. Find the **reciprocal** of 0.7. _____

13. How many **planes of symmetry** does a **cube** have? _____

14. What type of **transformation** is this?

    _____

15. **Reduce** this letter.   H   ☐

16. If a **circle** is divided into four equal **sectors**, what is the angle measure of each **segment**?

    _____

17. Express 40.0334 in **scientific notation**.

    _____

18. Express 1944 in **Roman numerals**.

    _____

19. $200 \times 0.007 =$ _____

20. The **distance** around a **circle** is known as the c_____.

Score: _____ /20 _____ %

Day 3

1. Evaluate 8^{-2}. _____
2. $2.5 + 0.05 =$ _____
3. $2.5 - 0.05 =$ _____
4. $2.5 \times 0.05 =$ _____
5. $2.5 \div 0.05 =$ _____
6. $^{1}/_{50}$ as a **decimal** is _____.
7. Solve the **equation** $7x < 2x + 5$. _____
8. What happens to the **angle measures** of a triangle when the triangle **increases** in size by a **scale** of two?

_____

9. $^{1}/_{4} \times$ _____ $= 21$
10. Name this **shape**.

_____

11. What is the **value** of y on this **number line**?

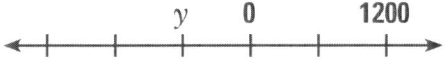

_____

12. Find the **reciprocal** of 0.8. _____
13. This **tetrahedron** has _____-fold **rotational symmetry**.

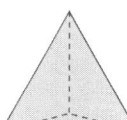

14. If a room is twice as long as it is wide and its **perimeter** is 600 m, what is its **width**?

_____

15. If a **circle** is divided into nine equal **sectors**, what is the angle measure of each **segment**?

_____

16. If a car travels a **distance** of 1000 km at 100 km/h, how long will the journey take?

_____

17. Express 0.03034 in **scientific notation**.

_____

18. Express 1942 in **Roman numerals**.

_____

19. $200 \times 0.008 =$ _____
20. What are **coordinates** plotted on?

_____

Day 4

1. Evaluate 2^{-6}. _____
2. $4.5 + 0.05 =$ _____
3. $4.5 - 0.05 =$ _____
4. $4.5 \times 0.05 =$ _____
5. $4.5 \div 0.05 =$ _____
6. $^{1}/_{20}$ as a **decimal** is _____.
7. **Factor**, then **evaluate** $12 \times 6 + 12 \times 2$.

_____

8. What happens to the **angle measures** of a triangle when the triangle **decreases** in size by a **scale** of two? _____

9. $^{1}/_{4} \times$ _____ $= 42$
10. In **triangles**, SSS is a condition for:

(a) congruency　(b) similarity　(c) both

11. What is the value of z on this **number line**?

_____

12. Find the **reciprocal** of 0.9. _____
13. This **shape** has _____-fold **rotational symmetry**.

14. If a room is twice as long as it is wide and its **perimeter** is 12,000 yd, what is its **width**?

_____

15. If a **circle** is divided into 36 equal **sectors**, what is the angle measure of each **segment**?

_____

16. If a car travels a **distance** of 1000 miles at 50 mph, how long will the journey take?

_____

17. Express 0.000334 in **scientific notation**.

_____

18. Express 1939 in **Roman numerals**.

_____

19. $200 \times 0.009 =$ _____
20. How many **quadrants** does a Cartesian plane have? _____

Score: _____ /20 _____ %

Score: _____ /20 _____ %

Day 1

1. Evaluate 9^{-2}. _____

2. $5.4 + 0.06 =$ _____

3. $5.4 - 0.06 =$ _____

4. $5.4 \times 0.06 =$ _____

5. $5.4 \div 0.06 =$ _____

6. $^5/_8$ as a **decimal** is _____.

7. The **product** of 0.5 and 0.6 is _____.

8. Name any **decimal** between $^1/_2$ and $^1/_4$ *(to two decimal places)*.

   _____

9. $^1/_4 \times$ _____ $= 13$

10. If a **circle** is divided into 12 equal **sectors**, what is the angle measure of each **segment**?

    _____

11. What is the **value** of a on this **number line**?

    _____

12. $(4 \times 2)^2 =$ _____

13. This **shape** has _____ -fold **rotational symmetry**.

    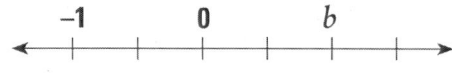

14. If Jia Xin's **average** after three tests is 96%, what must she score on her next test to make her average 97%? _____

15. If a field is twice as long as it is wide and its **perimeter** is 300 m, what is its **width**? _____

16. Find the tenth number in the **sequence**.

    18, 11, 4, ... _____

17. Express 0.01001 in **scientific notation**.

    _____

18. Express 1935 in **Roman numerals**.

    _____

19. $200 \times 0.010 =$ _____

20. Solve $\sqrt{(-3)^2 + (-4)^2}$.

    _____

Day 2

1. Evaluate $2\sqrt{9} + 2\sqrt{16}$. _____

2. $60 + 0.06 =$ _____

3. $60 - 0.06 =$ _____

4. $60 \times 0.06 =$ _____

5. $60 \div 0.06 =$ _____

6. $^7/_8$ as a **decimal** is _____.

7. $(^2/_3)^2 =$ _____

8. Write $^{64}/_6$ as a simplified **mixed numeral**.

   _____

9. $^3/_4 \times$ _____ $= 39$

10. If a **circle** is divided into three equal **sectors**, what is the angle measure of each **segment**?

    _____

11. What is the **value** of b on this **number line**?

12. $0.7 + ^3/_{10} =$ _____

13. How many **lines of symmetry** does a **rectangle** have? _____

14. If McKenzie's **average** after three tests is 83%, what must he score on his next test to make his average 85%?

    _____

15. If a paddock is twice as long as it is wide and its **perimeter** is 1800 yards, what is its **width**?

    _____

16. Find the tenth number in this **sequence**.

    19, 12, 5, ... _____

17. Express 401.0334 in **scientific notation**.

    _____

18. Express 1945 in **Roman numerals**.

    _____

19. $300 \times 0.001 =$ _____

20. **Factor** $49y^2 - 7x^2$. _____

Score: _____ /20 _____ %

Score: _____ /20 _____ %

Day 3

1. Evaluate 10^{-2}. _____

2. $1.2 + 0.06 =$ _____

3. $1.2 - 0.06 =$ _____

4. $1.2 \times 0.06 =$ _____

5. $1.2 \div 0.06 =$ _____

6. $^1/_8$ as a **decimal** is _____.

7. $(+3) - (-4) =$ _____

8. If a car travels at an **average speed** of 100 km/h, how long does it take to travel 200 km?

   _____

9. $^1/_4 \times$ _____ $= 11$

10. In this **sector graph**, how many students were surveyed if 24 chose swimming?

    _____

    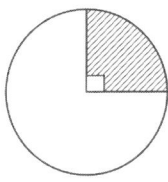

     $= swimming$

11. $1 \div {^1/_3} =$ _____

12. This **shape** has _____ -fold **rotational symmetry**.

13. If a **circle** is divided into two equal **sectors**, what is the angle measure of each **segment**?

    _____

14. If an **enclosure** is twice as long as it is wide and its **perimeter** is 1200 m, what is its **width**?

    _____

15. If Tahira's **average** after two tests is 69%, what must she score on her next test to make her average 72%? _____

16. Find the tenth number in the **sequence**.

    20, 13, 6, … _____

17. **Round** 6.3200 to three significant digits.

    _____

18. Express 1920 in **Roman numerals**.

    _____

19. $300 \times 0.002 =$ _____

20. How many **dozen** are there in 1344? _____

Score: /20 %

Day 4

1. Evaluate $3\sqrt{16} + \sqrt{16}$. _____

2. $2.4 + 0.06 =$ _____

3. $2.4 - 0.06 =$ _____

4. $2.4 \times 0.06 =$ _____

5. $2.4 \div 0.06 =$ _____

6. $^3/_8$ as a **decimal** is _____.

7. $(+3) + (-4) =$ _____

8. A car travels at an **average** speed of 60 mph. How long does it take to travel 240 miles?

   _____

9. $^3/_4 \times$ _____ $= 33$

10. In this **sector graph**, how many students were surveyed if eight played soccer?

    _____

    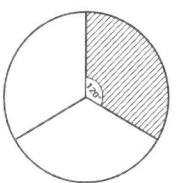

    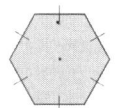 $= soccer$

11. The **reciprocal** of three is _____.

12. This **shape** has _____ -fold **rotational symmetry**.

13. If a **circle** is divided into 72 equal **sectors**, what is the angle measure of each **segment**?

    _____

14. If a hall is twice as long as it is wide and its **perimeter** is 1800 m, what is its **width**?

    _____

15. If Olympia's **average** after four tests is 88%, what must she score on her next test to make her average 90%? _____

16. Find the tenth number in the **sequence**.

    17, 10, 3, … _____

17. **Round** 6.020 to three significant digits.

    _____

18. Express 1930 in **Roman numerals**.

    _____

19. $300 \times 0.003 =$ _____

20. How many **dozen** are there in 1356? _____

Score: /20 %

Week 17

Day 1

1. Evaluate 11^{-2}. _____

2. $4.2 + 0.06 =$ _____

3. $4.2 - 0.06 =$ _____

4. $4.2 \times 0.06 =$ _____

5. $4.2 \div 0.06 =$ _____

6. $^3/_8$ as a **percentage** is _____.

7. Solve for x if $x^2 = 16$. _____

8. Factor $a(a - 2) + 3(a - 2)$.

   _____

9. $^1/_5 \times$ _____ $= 60$

10. Averaging a **speed** of 80 mph, a train travels from one city to another in 120 minutes. What is the **distance** between the cities?

    _____

11. 50% of 200 is _____.

12. An SAS **triangle** meets the requirements for:

    (a) congruency

    (b) similarity

    (c) both.

13. **Rotate** this image 90° counterclockwise.

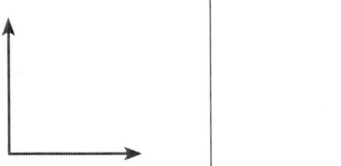

14. Complete the **pattern**. $^1/_{25}$, $^1/_5$, 1, 5, _____, _____

15. If a **circle** is divided into six equal **sectors**, what is the angle measure of each **segment**? _____

16. Find the tenth number in the **sequence**.

    15, 8, 1, … _____

17. **Round** 63.320 to three significant digits. _____

18. Express 1940 in **Roman numerals**.

    _____

19. $300 \times 0.006 =$ _____

20. How many **dozen** are there in 1368? _____

Day 2

1. Evaluate $\sqrt{25} + \sqrt{36}$. _____

2. $3.6 + 0.06 =$ _____

3. $3.6 - 0.06 =$ _____

4. $3.6 \times 0.06 =$ _____

5. $3.6 \div 0.06 =$ _____

6. $^5/_8$ as a **percentage** is _____.

7. $44 \times 25 =$ _____

8. Factor $4y(y - 3) - 4(y - 3)$.

   _____

9. $^1/_5 \times$ _____ $= 25$

10. Averaging 200 km/h, a train travels between two cities in 30 minutes. Find the **distance** between the cities. _____

11. 5% of 200 is _____.

12. In **triangles** the **RHS** property is a condition for:

    (a) congruency

    (b) similarity

    (c) both.

13. **Reflect** this image.

14. Complete the **pattern**. $^1/_{16}$, $^1/_4$, 1, 4, _____, _____

15. If a **circle** is divided into 12 equal **sectors**, what is the angle measure of each **segment**?

    _____

16. Find the tenth number in the **sequence**.

    14, 12, 10, … _____

17. **Round** 63,200 to three significant digits.

    _____

18. Express 1960 in **Roman numerals**.

    _____

19. $300 \times 0.007 =$ _____

20. How many **dozen** are there in 1380? _____

Score: _____ /20 _____ %

Score: _____ /20 _____ %

Day 3

1. Evaluate 12^{-2}. _____

2. $1.6 + 0.08 =$ _____

3. $1.6 - 0.08 =$ _____

4. $1.6 \times 0.08 =$ _____

5. $1.6 \div 0.08 =$ _____

6. $^7/_8$ as a **percentage** is _____.

7. For a **cube** to hold exactly one liter, what **length** do it **sides** have to be?

   _____

8. Which is **larger**?   (a) $^1/_4$ (b) 23.9%

9. $^1/_5 \times$ _____ = 15

10. Find the **value** of $10x$ if $x = -2$. _____

11. 5% of 2000 is _____.

12. In **triangles**, the **ASA** property is a condition for:

    (a) congruency

    (b) similarity

    (c) both.

13. To **enlarge** a shape is to _____ its size.

14. What is a **manometer** used to measure?

    _____

15. On a map, the **distance** from Dogtown to Fishville is 30 cm. If the scale is 1 : 5000, what is the actual **distance**?

    _____

16. Find the tenth number in the **sequence**.

    19, 16, 13, … _____

17. **Round** 2009 to three significant digits.

    _____

18. Express 1970 in **Roman numerals**.

    _____

19. $300 \times 0.004 =$ _____

20. How many **dozen** are there in 1392?

    _____

Score: _____ /20 _____ %

Day 4

1. Evaluate $\sqrt{64} + \sqrt{81}$. _____

2. $8 + 0.08 =$ _____

3. $8 - 0.08 =$ _____

4. $8 \times 0.08 =$ _____

5. $8 \div 0.08 =$ _____

6. $^1/_{20}$ as a **percentage** is _____.

7. $\sqrt{36 \div 4} =$ _____

8. Which is **larger**?   (a) $^2/_5$ (b) 40.1%

9. $^1/_5 \times$ _____ = 18

10. Find the **value** of $8b$ if $2b = -3$. _____

11. **Fifty percent** of 20 is _____.

12. In **triangles**, AA is a condition for:

    (a) congruency

    (b) similarity

    (c) both.

13. To **reduce** a shape is to _____ its size.

14. If a **circle** is divided into 18 equal **sectors**, what is the angle measure of each **segment**?

    _____

15. The **distance** between Valencia and Pasco is 10 in. on a map. If the scale is 1 : 150,000, what is the actual **distance**?

    _____

16. Find the tenth number in the **sequence**.

    19, 15, 11, … _____

17. **Round** 2004 to three significant digits.

    _____

18. Express 1980 in **Roman numerals**.

    _____

19. $300 \times 0.005 =$ _____

20. How many **dozen** are there in 1404?

    _____

Score: _____ /20 _____ %

Day 1

1. Evaluate 3^{-3}. _____

2. $6.4 + 0.08 =$ _____

3. $6.4 - 0.08 =$ _____

4. $6.4 \times 0.08 =$ _____

5. $6.4 \div 0.08 =$ _____

6. $\frac{1}{25}$ as a **percentage** is _____.

7. During a 35%-reduction book sale, how much would an $8 book **cost**?

   _____

8. $\frac{3}{7} - \frac{1}{3} =$ _____

9. $\frac{1}{5} \times$ _____ $= 20$

10. **Simplify** and rewrite the expression $7 \div g + 4 \div 5$. _____

11. Five **percent** of 20 is _____.

12. $275 \div 11 =$ _____

13. A cone cut **horizontally** produces a _____ **cross section**.

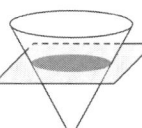

14. If a **circle** is divided into 36 equal **sectors**, what is the angle measure of each **segment**?

    _____

15. **Convert** 9391 centimeters to meters.

    _____

16. Find the tenth number in the **sequence**.
    19, 11, 3, … _____

17. **Round** 6.3200 to three significant digits.

    _____

18. Express 2010 in **Roman numerals**.

    _____

19. $300 \times 0.006 =$ _____

20. How many **dozen** are there in 1416?

    _____

Day 2

1. Evaluate $\sqrt{5} \times \sqrt{2}$. _____

2. $4.8 + 0.08 =$ _____

3. $4.8 - 0.08 =$ _____

4. $4.8 \times 0.08 =$ _____

5. $4.8 \div 0.08 =$ _____

6. $\frac{1}{40}$ as a **percentage** is _____.

7. During a 35%-reduction book sale, how much would a $6 book **cost**?

   _____

8. $\frac{8}{5} - \frac{1}{10} =$ _____

9. $\frac{1}{5} \times$ _____ $= 125$

10. **Simplify** and rewrite the expression $a \div 6 + 7 \times t$. _____

11. 10% of 20 is _____.

12. $264 \div 11 =$ _____

13. A cone cut **vertically** produces an _____ -shaped **cross section**.

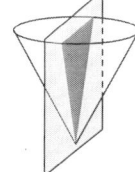

14. If a **circle** is divided into 10 equal **sectors**, what is the angle measure of each **segment**?

    _____

15. **Convert** 9139 centimeters to meters.

    _____

16. Find the tenth number in the **sequence**.
    19, 14, 9, … _____

17. **Round** 63,200 to three significant digits.

    _____

18. Express 2001 in **Roman numerals**.

    _____

19. $300 \times 0.007 =$ _____

20. How many **dozen** are there in 1428?

    _____

Score: /20   %   Score: /20   %

Day 3

1. Evaluate 3^{-4}. _____

2. $4.5 + 0.08 =$ _____

3. $4.5 - 0.08 =$ _____

4. $4.5 \times 0.08 =$ _____

5. $4.5 \div 0.08$ (as a **fraction**) = _____

6. $\frac{1}{50}$ as a **percentage** is _____.

7. Express 175 as a **product** of **prime numbers** in **exponent form**.

_____

8. Solve for x if $x/4 - 1 = 3$. _____

9. $\frac{1}{5} \times$ _____ $= 120$

10. **Convert** 231.9 centimeters to meters.

_____

11. $\frac{1}{5} + 0.8 =$ _____

12. Complete the **pattern**.

0.5, 0.7, 1.1, 1.7, _____, _____

13. A cone cut **obliquely** produces an _____ **cross section**.

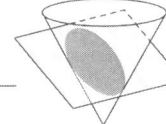

14. If a **circle** is divided into 20 equal **sectors**, what is the angle measure of each **segment**?

_____

15. If Royce's **average** after three tests is 85%, what must he score on his next test to make his average 88%?

_____

16. $253 \div 11 =$ _____

17. **Round** 46.3200 to two significant digits.

_____

18. Express 2009 in **Roman numerals**.

_____

19. $300 \times 0.008 =$ _____

20. How many **dozen** are there in 1440?

_____

Day 4

1. Evaluate 2^{-1}. _____

2. $5.6 + 0.08 =$ _____

3. $5.6 - 0.08 =$ _____

4. $5.6 \times 0.08 =$ _____

5. $5.6 \div 0.08 =$ _____

6. $\frac{1}{100}$ as a **percentage** is _____.

7. Express 180 as a **product** of **prime numbers** in **exponent form**.

_____

8. Solve for x if $2(x/5) = 4$. _____

9. $\frac{1}{5} \times$ _____ $= 80$

10. **Convert** 23.19 centimeters to meters.

_____

11. $0.75 \times 3 =$ _____

12. Complete the **pattern**.

0.4, 0.6, 1.0, 1.6, _____, _____

13. A cone cut **vertically** *not* through the center produces _____ _____ as a **cross section**.

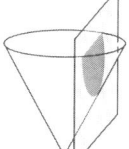

14. If a **circle** is divided into four equal **sectors**, what is the angle measure of each **segment**?

_____

15. If Ash's **average** after three tests is 78%, what must he score on his next test to make his average 80%?

_____

16. $242 \div 11 =$ _____

17. **Round** 46,320 to two significant digits.

_____

18. Express 2011 in **Roman numerals**.

_____

19. $300 \times 0.009 =$ _____

20. How many **dozen** are there in 1452?

_____

Score: ___ /20 ___ %

Score: ___ /20 ___ %

Week 19

Day 1

1. **Evaluate** 5^{-3}. _____
2. $2.4 + 0.08 =$ _____
3. $2.4 - 0.08 =$ _____
4. $2.4 \times 0.08 =$ _____
5. $2.4 \div 0.08 =$ _____
6. $^1/_{200}$ as a **percentage** is _____.
7. Today's date in **international standard date** notation is ___YYYY__ / __MM__ / __DD__.
8. Solve for x if $x^2 = 81$. _____
9. $^1/_5 \times$ _____ $= 8$
10. **Convert** 1.039 centimeters to meters.

    _____
11. $^3/_5 + 0.4 =$ _____
12. Complete the **pattern.**

    2.0, 1.9, 1.7, _____, _____, _____
13. A cone cut **diagonally** and **parallel to its slope** produces a

    _____

    -shaped **cross section.**
14. Complete the **pattern:**

    0.2, 0.4, 0.8, _____, _____, _____
15. If a **circle** is divided into five equal **sectors**, what is the angle measure of each **segment?**

    _____
16. $11 \times 11 =$ _____
17. **Round** 61.99 to three significant digits.

    _____
18. Express 2020 in **Roman numerals.**

    _____
19. $300 \times 0.01 =$ _____
20. How many **dozen** are there in 1464?

    _____

Score: /20   %

Day 2

1. If $3^a = {}^1/_9$, then $a =$ _____.
2. $3.2 + 0.08 =$ _____
3. $3.2 - 0.08 =$ _____
4. $3.2 \times 0.08 =$ _____
5. $3.2 \div 0.08 =$ _____
6. $^1/_{1000}$ as a **percentage** is _____.
7. During a 35%-reduction book sale, how much would a $5 book **cost?**

    _____
8. Solve for x if $x^3 = 27$. _____
9. $^1/_5 \times$ _____ $= 0.8$
10. **Convert** 1.939 centimeters to meters.

    _____
11. $3^5/3^5 =$ _____
12. Complete the **pattern.**

    1, 8, 27, 64, _____, _____
13. Is this a **parabola** or a **hyperbola** shape?

    (a) parabola

    (b) hyperbola
14. Complete the **pattern.**

    0.3, 0.6, 1.2, _____, _____, _____
15. If a **circle** is divided into 120 equal **sectors**, what is the angle measure of each **segment?**

    _____
16. $12 \times 11 =$ _____
17. **Round** 6.3200 to three significant digits.

    _____
18. Express 2015 in **Roman numerals.**

    _____
19. $500 \times 0.001 =$ _____
20. How many **dozen** are there in 1476?

    _____

Score: /20   %

Day 3

1. Evaluate 2^{-2}. _____
2. $300 + 0.01 =$ _____
3. $300 - 0.01 =$ _____
4. $300 \times 0.01 =$ _____
5. $300 \div 0.01 =$ _____
6. $^1/_{10,000}$ as a **percentage** is _____.
7. Solve for x. $2x + 5 = 11$ _____
8. Express 144 as a product of **prime numbers** in **exponent form.** _____.
9. $^1/_5 \times$ _____ $= 10$
10. **Convert** 732 centimeters to meters.

    _____
11. $3^0 =$ _____
12. Complete the **pattern.**

    $0.1, 1.0, 10,$ _____, _____, _____
13. Cutting a **cube** vertically parallel to any face produces a _____ -shaped **cross section.**

14. If a **circle** is divided into eight equal **sectors**, what is the angle measure of each **segment**?

    _____
15. If Ben's **average** after three tests is 77%, what must he score on his next test to make his average 80%?

    _____
16. Complete the **pattern.**

    $1, 4, 9,$ _____, _____, _____
17. **Round** 632.98 to three significant digits.

    _____
18. Express 2016 in **Roman numerals.**

    _____
19. $3 - 0.5 =$ _____
20. How many **dozen** are there in 1488?

    _____

Score: _____ /20 _____ %

Day 4

1. Evaluate 2^{-3}. _____
2. $400 + 0.001 =$ _____
3. $400 - 0.001 =$ _____
4. $400 \times 0.001 =$ _____
5. $400 \div 0.001 =$ _____
6. $^1/_{12}$ as a **percentage** is _____.
7. Solve for x if $3x - 4 = 2$. _____
8. Express 120 as a **product** of **prime numbers** in **exponent form.** _____.
9. $^1/_5 \times$ _____ $= 1$
10. **Convert** 198 centimeters to meters.

    _____
11. $4^0 =$ _____
12. Complete the **pattern.**

    $100, 10, 1,$ _____, _____, _____
13. Cutting a **cube** horizontally parallel to any face produces a _____ -shaped **cross section.**

14. If a **circle** is divided into 45 equal **sectors**, what is the angle measure of each **segment**?

    _____
15. If Hannah's **average** after three tests is 59%, what must she score on her next test to make her average 65%?

    _____
16. Complete the **pattern.**

    $1, 3, 6,$ _____, _____, _____
17. **Round** 606.3200 to three significant digits.

    _____
18. Express 2022 in **Roman numerals.**

    _____
19. $4 - 0.6 =$ _____
20. How many **dozen** are there in 1500?

    _____

Score: _____ /20 _____ %

Day 1

1. Evaluate 2^{-4}. _____

2. $20 + 0.03 =$ _____

3. $20 - 0.03 =$ _____

4. $20 \times 0.03 =$ _____

5. $20 \div 0.03 =$ _____

6. $\frac{1}{20}$ as a **percentage** is _____.

7. Solve for c if $4 = 2c + 2$. _____

8. Solve for x if $5x - 5 = 25$. _____

9. $\frac{1}{5} \times$ _____ $= 24$

10. **Convert** 939 centimeters to meters. _____

11. Complete the **pattern**.

    0.2, 0.4, 0.6, _____, _____, _____

12. $(-5) + (+4) =$ _____

13. Cutting a **cube** from one edge to another produces a _____ **cross section**.

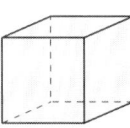

14. $13 \times 11 =$ _____

15. If a **circle** is divided into 10 equal **sectors**, what is the angle measure of each **segment**?

    _____

16. Complete the **pentagonal number pattern**.

    1, 5, 12, _____, _____

17. **Round** 6.3272 to three significant digits.

    _____

18. Express 2023 in **Roman numerals**.

    _____

19. $3 - 0.5 =$ _____

20. How many **dozen** are there in 1512?

    _____

Day 2

1. Evaluate 2^{-5}. _____

2. $20 + 0.02 =$ _____

3. $20 - 0.02 =$ _____

4. $20 \times 0.02 =$ _____

5. $20 \div 0.02 =$ _____

6. $\frac{1}{5}$ as a **percentage** is _____.

7. Solve for x if $9 = 2x + 5$. _____

8. Solve for x if $5x - 2 = 58$. _____

9. $\frac{1}{5} \times$ _____ $= 23$

10. **Convert** 931 centimeters to meters. _____

11. Complete the **pattern**.

    0.3, 0.6, 0.9, _____, _____, _____

12. $(+5) - (+4) =$ _____

13. Cutting an edge off a **cube** produces a _____ **cross section**.

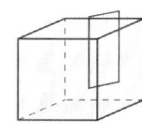

14. $15 \times 11 =$ _____

15. If a **circle** is divided into six equal **sectors**, what is the angle measure of each **segment**?

    _____

16. Complete the **hexagonal number pattern**.

    1, 6, 15, 28, _____, _____

17. **Round** 6.3250 to three significant digits.

    _____

18. Express 2013 in **Roman numerals**.

    _____

19. $4 - 0.6 =$ _____

20. How many **dozen** are there in 1524?

    _____

Score: _____ /20 _____ %

Score: _____ /20 _____ %

Day 3

1. Express 2^{-6} as a **fraction**. _____

2. $0.20 + 0.03 =$ _____

3. $0.20 - 0.03 =$ _____

4. $0.20 \times 0.03 =$ _____

5. $0.20 \div 0.03$ as a **fraction** is _____.

6. $^1/_{40}$ as a **percentage** is _____.

7. Find the **simple interest** on $1000 invested at a rate of 7% **per annum** for three years.

_____

8. **Convert** $^2/_5$ of one kilometer into meters. _____

9. $^1/_5 \times$ _____ $= 40$

10. $(-4) \times (-2k) =$ _____

11. $(3^2 + 2)^2 =$ _____

12. Sabrina doubled the quantities of her punch by the **ratio** of two cups of orange juice to three cups of cranberry juice to three cups of ginger ale. Write the **ratio** she uses.

_____

13. Cutting one corner of a **cube** produces a _____ **cross section**.
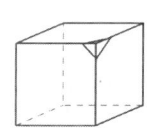

14. If Callie was paid $28.50 for three hours work, what was her **hourly rate**?

_____

15. If a **circle** is divided into 60 equal **sectors**, what is the angle measure of each **segment**?

_____

16. $^{187}/_{11} =$ _____

17. **Round** 56.012 to four significant digits.

_____

18. Express 2029 in **Roman numerals**.

_____

19. If $x = 2^2$, find the **value** of $4x - 6$. _____

20. How many **dozen** are there in 1536? _____

Score: /20   %

Day 4

1. Express 2^{-7} as a **fraction**. _____

2. $0.20 + 0.002 =$ _____

3. $0.20 - 0.002 =$ _____

4. $0.20 \times 0.002 =$ _____

5. $0.20 \div 0.002 =$ _____

6. $^1/_{25}$ as a **percentage** is _____.

7. Find the **simple interest** on $1000 invested at a rate of 6% **per annum** for two years.

_____

8. **Convert** $^3/_5$ of 10 kilometers into meters. _____

9. $^1/_5 \times$ _____ $= 2.5$

10. $(-2) \times (-5r) =$ _____

11. $(3^2 + 4)^2 =$ _____

12. Hermoine doubled the quantity of her cookie recipe by the **ratio** of 100 g finest chocolate, 20 g marshmallows, and 100 g coconut. Write the **ratio** of the amounts she used.

_____

13. Cutting a **cylinder** horizontally produces a _____ **cross section**.
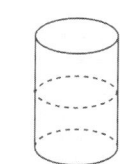

14. If Sabine was **paid** $11.50 an hour, how much was she paid after working for $4^1/_2$ hours?

_____

15. If a **circle** is divided into 90 equal **sectors**, what is the angle measure of each **segment**?

_____

16. $^{209}/_{11} =$ _____

17. **Round** 5.6012 to three significant digits.

_____

18. Express 2032 in **Roman numerals**.

_____

19. $3 - 0.05 =$ _____

20. How many **dozen** are there in 1548? _____

Score: /20   %

Day 1

1. **Evaluate** 2^{-4}. _____
2. $0.08 + 0.50 + 0.64 + 0.42 =$ _____
3. $3 - 0.5 =$ _____
4. $20 \times 0.03 =$ _____
5. $\$17.50 \div 2 =$ _____
6. $^1/_{50}$ as a **percentage** is _____.
7. Which is **greater**, 0.6 or 0.06?   (a) 0.6   (b) 0.06
8. If Liann **saves** \$40 per week, how much does she save each year?

   _____
9. $^1/_5 \times$ _____ $= 12.5$
10. $15^2 =$ _____
11. What is the **value** of 4 in 65,304,219?

    _____
12. Write 100% as a **fraction** in its simplest form.

    _____
13. A **cylinder** cut obliquely produces what shape **cross section**?

    _____
14. List the **common elements** in the **multisets** [S, o, p, h, i, e] and [S, a, r, a, h].

    _____
15. This **shape** is called a _____ of a **circle**.
16. $^{-18}/_{-3} =$ _____
17. **Round** 896.3200 to three significant digits.

    _____
18. Express 2024 in **Roman numerals**.

    _____
19. $4 - 0.015 =$ _____
20. How many **dozen** are there in 1560?

    _____

Day 2

1. **Evaluate** 2^{-5}. _____
2. $0.8 + 0.7 =$ _____
3. $4 - 0.6 =$ _____
4. $20 \times 0.02 =$ _____
5. $\$5.00 \div 4 =$ _____
6. $^1/_{20}$ as a **percentage** is _____.
7. Which is **greater**? (a) 0.16 or (b) 0.061
8. During a 35%-reduction book sale, how much would a \$22 book **cost**?

   _____
9. $^1/_5 \times$ _____ $= 21$
10. $17^2 =$ _____
11. What is the **value** of 5 in 59,876,432?

    _____
12. Write 110% as a **fraction** in its simplest form.

    _____
13. A **cylinder** cut vertically produces what shape **cross section**?

    _____
14. List the **common elements** in the **sets** [t, i, g, e, r] and [l, i, o, n].

    _____
15. This **shape** is called a _____ of a **circle**.
16. $^{-35}/_7 =$ _____
17. **Round** 8.96609 to three significant digits.

    _____
18. Express 2055 in **Roman numerals**.

    _____
19. The next **prime number** after 7 is _____.
20. How many **dozen** are there in 1572?

    _____

Score:	/20	%	Score:	/20	%

Day 3

1. Evaluate 2^{-6}. _____

2. $0.92 + 0.97 + 0.98 =$ _____

3. $3 - 0.05 =$ _____

4. $0.20 \times 0.03 =$ _____

5. $5 \div 100 =$ _____

6. $^1/_{16}$ as a **percentage** is _____.

7. List the **common elements** in the **multisets** [s, e, v ,e, n] and [n, i, n, e].

   _____

8. During a 35%-reduction book sale, how much would a $28 book **cost**?

   _____

9. $^1/_5 \times$ _____ $= 3$

10. $20^2 =$ _____

11. What is the **value** of 9 in 8,390,217?

    _____

12. Write 25% as a **fraction** in its simplest form.

    _____

13. What formula is used to calculate the **area** of an **ellipse**?

    _____

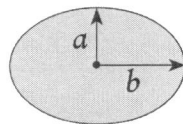

14. Line a is called a

    _____.

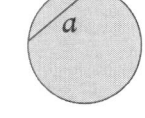

15. The **sum** of these two shaded regions equals

    _____.

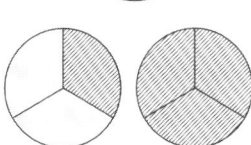

16. $^{24}/_{-8} =$ _____

17. **Round** 10,060 to three significant digits.

    _____

18. **Multiply** 5^2 by 4. _____

19. The next **prime number** after 31 is _____.

20. If $x = 12$, find the value of $3x - 16$. _____

Score: _____ /20   _____ %

Day 4

1. Evaluate 2^{-7}. _____

2. $0.91 + 0.99 =$ _____

3. $4 - 0.005 =$ _____

4. $0.20 \times 0.002 =$ _____

5. $5 \div 1 =$ _____

6. $^1/_{15}$ as a **percentage** is _____.

7. List the **common elements** in the **multisets** [t, e, n] and [n, i, n, e].

   _____

8. During a 35%-reduction book sale, how much would a $34 book **cost**?

   _____

9. $^1/_5 \times$ _____ $= 7$

10. $25^2 =$ _____

11. What is the **value** of 7 in 10,304,719?

    _____

12. Write 20% as a **fraction** in its simplest form.

    _____

13. What formula is used to calculate the **volume** of a **trapezoidal prism**?

    _____

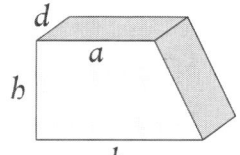

14. Line a is called the

    _____ of the **circle**.

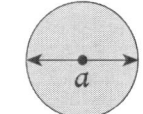

15. The **sum** of these two shaded regions equals

    _____.

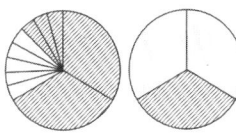

16. **Twenty-five percent** of eight hours = _____

17. **Round** 63,200 to two significant digits.

    _____

18. **Multiply** 5^2 by 5. _____

19. The next **prime number** after 41 is _____.

20. How many **dozen** are there in 1584? _____

Score: _____ /20   _____ %

Day 1

1. Evaluate 2^{-4}. _____
2. $0.99 + 0.11 =$ _____
3. $3 - 0.5 =$ _____
4. $20 \times 0.03 =$ _____
5. $5 \div 0.1 =$ _____
6. $^1/_{10}$ as a **percentage** is _____ .
7. List the **common elements** in the **multisets** [c, h, i, c, k, e, n] and [c, h, i, p, s].

   _____
8. When one kilogram of coal is burnt, 90 grams of ash remains. What **percentage** is this of the original amount? _____
9. $^1/_5 \times$ _____ $= 9$
10. $13^2 =$ _____
11. What is the **value** of 2 in 16,789,921?

    _____
12. Write $233^1/_3\%$ as a **fraction** in its simplest form.

    _____
13. The **formula** to calculate the **surface area** of a **sphere** is

    _____ .
14. Draw a **diameter** on this **circle**.
15. The **sum** of these three shaded regions equals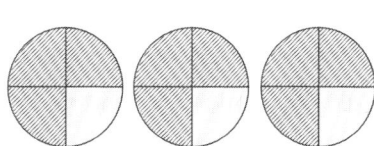

    _____ .
16. **Twenty-five percent** of four hours = _____
17. **Round** 63,297 to one significant digit.

    _____
18. **Multiply** 5^2 by 6. _____
19. **Square** 20 and **add** 22. _____
20. How many **dozen** are there in 1596? _____

Day 2

1. Evaluate 2^{-5}. _____
2. $2.11 + 0.44 + 0.55 =$ _____
3. $4 - 0.6 =$ _____
4. $20 \times 0.02 =$ _____
5. $5 \div 0.01 =$ _____
6. $^1/_{11}$ as a **percentage** is _____ .
7. List the **common elements** in the **multisets** [h, e, r, o, e, s] and [h, o, u, s, e].

   _____
8. The unit for measuring **thermodynamic temperature** is a

   _____ .
9. $^1/_5 \times$ _____ $= 13$
10. $16^2 =$ _____
11. What is the **value** of 1 in 65,314,289?

    _____
12. Write $333^1/_3\%$ as a **fraction** in its simplest form.

    _____
13. The **formula** to calculate the **volume** of a **sphere** is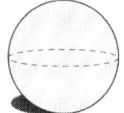

    _____ .
14. Draw a **radius** on this **circle**.
15. The **sum** of these two shaded regions equals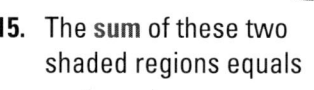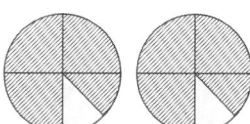

    _____ .
16. **Twenty-five percent** of two hours = _____
17. **Round** 6.3200 to one significant digit.

    _____
18. **Multiply** 5^2 by 8. _____
19. **Square** 25 and **add** 23. _____
20. How many **dozen** are there in 1608?

    _____

Score: _____ /20 _____ %   Score: _____ /20 _____ %

Day 3

1. Evaluate 2^{-6}. _____

2. $6.1 + 0.91 =$ _____

3. $3 - 0.05 =$ _____

4. $200 \times 0.0006 =$ _____

5. $5 \div 10 =$ _____

6. $\frac{1}{9}$ as a **percentage** is _____.

7. Simplify $\frac{6y^2}{9y^2}$. _____

8. List the **elements** in common for the **multisets** [b, r, o, t, h, e, r] and [s, i, s, t, e, r].

   _____

9. $\frac{1}{5} \times$ _____ $= 15$

10. $24^2 =$ _____

11. What is the **value** of 5 in 65,304,219?

    _____

12. Write 75% as a **fraction** in its simplest form.

    _____

13. The **formula** to calculate the **volume** of a **cylinder** is

    _____.

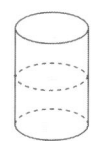

14. The **radius** of the **circle** is

    _____.

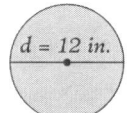

$d = 12$ in.

15. Todd, Britt, and Ryan share a pizza in the **ratio** 1 : 2 : 3. If Britt's share is 200 ounces, what is the total **weight** of the pizza?

    _____

16. **Twenty-five percent** of one hour in minutes is _____.

17. **Round** 6.3200 to four significant digits.

    _____

18. The next **prime number** after 101 is _____.

19. **Square** 15 and **add** 21. _____

20. If $x = 4$, find the value of $4x - 6$. _____

Day 4

1. Evaluate 2^{-7}. _____

2. $3.3 + 1.4 =$ _____

3. $4 - 0.005 =$ _____

4. $0.20 \times 0.002 =$ _____

5. $5 \div 20 =$ _____

6. $\frac{1}{20}$ as a **percentage** is _____.

7. If a plumber charges $120 for three hours of work, what is his **hourly rate**?

   _____

8. List the **elements** in common for the **multisets** [a, u, n, t] and [u, n, c, l, e].

   _____

9. $\frac{1}{5} \times$ _____ $= 16$

10. $19^2 =$ _____

11. What is the **value** of 8 in 65,804,219?

    _____

12. Write 55% as a **fraction** in its simplest form.

    _____

13. The **formula** for calculating the **volume** of a **triangular prism** is

    _____.

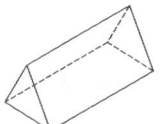

14. The **diameter** of the **circle** is

    _____

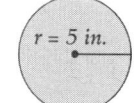

$r = 5$ in.

15. Find the value of $x°$ if $3x° = 45°$.

    _____

16. **Twenty-five percent** of 30 minutes is _____.

17. **Round** 6.3209 to four significant digits.

    _____

18. The next **prime number** after 103 is _____.

19. **Square** 11 and **add** 2. _____

20. How many **dozen** are there in 1620? _____

Score: _____ /20 _____ %

Score: _____ /20 _____ %

Week 23

Day 1

1. Evaluate 2^{-4}. _____

2. $1.035 + 2.987 =$ _____

3. $3 - 0.7 =$ _____

4. $30 \times 0.03 =$ _____

5. $0.8 \div 0.08 =$ _____

6. $^1/_{200}$ as a **percentage** is _____.

7. A shirt is 40% polyester and the rest is cotton. Express this as a **ratio**. _____

8. List the **elements** in common for the **sets** [b, e, c, k, s] and [p, o, s, h].

    _____

9. $^1/_5 \times$ _____ $= 6$

10. $18^2 =$ _____

11. What is the **value** of 9 in 65,304,219?

    _____

12. Write 45% as a **fraction** in its simplest form.

    _____

13. The **formula** to **calculate** the **volume** of a cone is

    _____.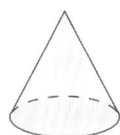

14. Give an example of a **perfect number**.

    _____

15. $^2/_9$ as a **recurring decimal** is _____.

16. **Twenty-five percent** of 12 hours = _____

17. If Kamal is **paid** $240 for 20 hours work, how much would he receive for 12 hours of work?

    _____

18. **Round** 63.290 to three significant digits.

    _____

19. $40 \times 0.02 =$ _____

20. How many **dozen** are there in 1632?

    _____

Day 2

1. Evaluate 3^{-4}. _____

2. $0.518 + 5.18 =$ _____

3. $7 - 1.6 =$ _____

4. $30 \times 0.02 =$ _____

5. $0.7 \div 0.07 =$ _____

6. $^1/_2$ as a **percentage** is _____.

7. Nitric acid is 20% hydrogen, 20% nitrogen, and the rest oxygen. Express this as a **ratio**.

    _____

8. List the **elements** in common for the **multisets** [e, d, w, a, r, d] and [b, e, l, l, a].

    _____

9. $^1/_5 \times$ _____ $= 8$

10. $14^2 =$ _____

11. What is the **value** of 4 in 65.304?

    _____

12. Write 65% as a **fraction** in its simplest form.

    _____

13. The **formula** to calculate the **volume** of a **triangular pyramid** is

    _____.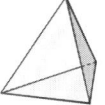

14. What is a **perfect number**?

    _____
    _____

15. $^3/_9$ as a **recurring decimal** is _____.

16. **Twenty-five percent** of 24 hours = _____

17. If Michael is **paid** $320 for 20 hours work, how much would he receive for eight hours of work?

    _____

18. **Round** 0.6329 to three significant digits.

    _____

19. **Square** 12 and **add** 12. _____

20. How many **dozen** are there in 1644?

    _____

Day 3

1. Convert 3^{-6} to a **fraction**. _____

2. $60.5 + 50.6 =$ _____

3. $6 - 0.3 =$ _____

4. $0.20 \times 0.03 =$ _____

5. $0.9 \div 0.09 =$ _____

6. $^4/_9$ as a **recurring decimal** is _____.

7. Today's date in **international standard date** notation is _____ / _____ / _____.
   (YYYY / MM / DD)

8. 110% of $250 is _____.

9. $^1/_5 \times$ _____ $= 12$

10. $\sqrt{169} =$ _____

11. What is the **value** of 4 in 6.5304219?

   _____

12. Write $16^2/_3\%$ as a **fraction** in its simplest form.

   _____

13. The **formula** to calculate the **volume** of a **cube** is

   _____.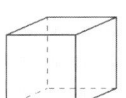

14. An ancient Greek instrument for observing celestial bodies was the a_____.

15. What three **translations** are needed to swap the ant with the bee?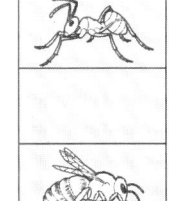

   _____,

   _____,

16. **Twenty-five percent** of 48 hours = _____

17. If Xin is **paid** $400 for 20 hours of work, how much would she receive for 14 hours of work?

   _____

18. **Round** 0.334 to one significant digit.

   _____

19. **Square** 13 and **add** 11. _____

20. If $x = 6$, find the value of $4x - 6$. _____

Day 4

1. Convert 3^{-7} to a **fraction**. _____

2. $40.5 + 50.4 =$ _____   3. $7 - 0.1 =$ _____

4. $0.20 \times 0.002 =$ _____

5. $0.6 \div 0.06 =$ _____

6. $^5/_9$ as a **percentage** is _____.

7. List the **elements** in common for the **multisets** [b, r, a, d] and [a, n, g, e, l, i, n, a]. _____

8. 110% of $500 is _____.

9. $^1/_5 \times$ _____ $= 14$

10. $\sqrt{256} =$ _____

11. What is the **value** of 4 in 653.04219?

   _____

12. Write $8^1/_3\%$ as a **fraction** in its simplest form.

   _____

13. The **formula** to calculate the **volume** of a **rectangular prism** is _____.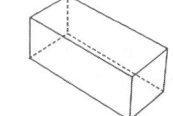

14. The value for **phi** (known as the **golden ratio**) to one decimal place is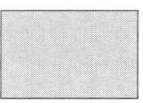

   _____.

15. Write the order of the eight **translations** needed to swap the star shapes with the moon shapes. *(Hint: Think: slide, jump, etc.)*

   _____

16. **Seventy-five percent** of 24 hours = _____

17. If Elise is **paid** $150 for 25 hours of work, how much would she receive for 12 hours of work?

   _____

18. **Round** 632 to one significant digit. _____

19. $4 - 0.6 =$ _____

20. How many **dozen** are there in 1656? _____

Score: _____ /20 _____ %   Score: _____ /20 _____ %

Day 1

1. **Evaluate** 4^{-4}. _____

2. $40 + 0.03 =$ _____

3. $40 - 0.03 =$ _____

4. $40 \times 0.03 =$ _____

5. $40 \div 0.03 =$ _____

6. $(+18) \div (-3) =$ _____

7. **Round** 1.99 to
   one **decimal** place. _____

8. List the **elements** in common for the **sets**
   [t, o, m] and [k, a, t, i, e].

   _____

9. $^1/_5 \times$ _____ $= 25$

10. Rewrite 0.0678 as a **percentage**. _____

11. What is the **value** of 5 in 6.5304219?

    _____

12. Write 10% as a **fraction** in its simplest form.

    _____

13. The **formula** to calculate the
    volume of a **rectangular**
    pyramid is

    _____.

14. $\sqrt{625} =$ _____

15. If a **deposit** of $750 earns 2.8% **compound interest**
    calculated monthly, how much money is in the
    account after three months?

    _____

16. Write $33^1/_3$% as a **fraction** in its simplest form.

    _____

17. If Cerys is **paid** $280 for 28 hours of work, how
    much would she receive for 12 hours of work?

    _____

18. **Round** 5.78 to two significant digits. _____

19. $8 - 0.005 =$ _____

20. How many **dozen** are there in 1668?

    _____

Score: ___ /20 ___ %

Day 2

1. **Evaluate** 5^{-5}. _____

2. $40 + 0.02 =$ _____

3. $40 - 0.02 =$ _____

4. $40 \times 0.02 =$ _____

5. $40 \div 0.02 =$ _____

6. $(+4) - (-4) =$ _____

7. **Round** 1.956 to
   one **decimal** place. _____

8. List the elements in common for [n, i, c, o, l, e]
   and [k, e, i, t, h].

   _____

9. $^1/_5 \times$ _____ $= 35$

10. Rewrite 0.0697 as a **percentage**. _____

11. What is the **place value** of 2 in 6.5304219?

    _____

12. Write 1% as a **fraction** in its simplest form.

    _____

13. The formula to calculate the
    volume of a square
    pyramid is

    _____.

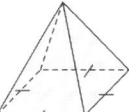

14. $\sqrt{529} =$ _____

15. Name the **quadrilateral** with only one pair of
    parallel sides.

    _____

16. Write $66^2/_3$% as a **fraction** in its simplest form.

    _____

17. If Mark is **paid** $24 for two hours of work, how
    much would he receive for 15 hours of work?

    _____

18. **Round** 65,730 to two significant digits.

    _____

19. $5 - 0.05 =$ _____

20. How many **dozen** are there in 1680?

    _____

Score: ___ /20 ___ %

Week 24

Day 3

1. Evaluate 2^6. _____
2. $0.20 + 0.03 =$ _____
3. $0.20 - 0.03 =$ _____
4. $0.20 \times 0.03 =$ _____
5. $0.20 \div 0.03 =$ _____
6. If angles $x°$ and $3x°$ are **supplementary**, what is the value of $x°$?

   _____

   0° $3x°$ / $x°$ 180°

7. **Round** 1.06 to one **decimal** place. _____
8. $\sqrt{289} =$ _____
9. $^1/_3 \times$ _____ $= 25$
10. Rewrite 0.0692 as a **percentage**. _____
11. The **value** of 1 in 6.5304219 is

    _____ .

12. Does every **isosceles triangle** have three axes of symmetry?   **Yes   No**
13. The **formula** to calculate the **volume** of any **pyramid** is _____ the area of the base multiplied by the _____ from the base to the apex.
14. The symbol $\nsubseteq$ means

    _____ .

15. What **angle** measure is its own **complement**?

    _____

16. **Seventy-five percent** of four hours =

    _____

17. **Round** 99.99 to two significant digits. _____
18. The next **prime number** after 11 is _____ .
19. **Square** 17 and **add** 22. _____
20. If $x = 9$, find the value of $4x - 6$. _____

Score: _____ /20 _____ %

Day 4

1. Evaluate 2^7. _____
2. $0.20 + 0.002 =$ _____
3. $0.20 - 0.002 =$ _____
4. $0.20 \times 0.002 =$ _____
5. $0.20 \div 0.002 =$ _____
6. If angles $a°$ and $2a°$ are **complementary**, what is the value of $a°$?

   _____

   $2a°$ / $a°$

7. **Round** 1.55 to one **decimal** place. _____
8. $\sqrt{144} =$ _____
9. $^1/_3 \times$ _____ $= 20$
10. Rewrite 0.0689 as a **percentage**. _____
11. The **value** of 9 in 6.5304219 is

    _____ .

12. Does every **square** have exactly two axes of symmetry?   **Yes   No**
13. The **volume** of any **prism** is **calculated** by multiplying the area of the _____ by the _____ .
14. The symbol $\cong$ means

    _____ .

15. In 2007, 15-year-old Max, born February 29, 1992, calculated the number of birthdays he had celebrated since the date of his birth. How many birthdays had he celebrated?

    _____

16. **Seventy-five percent** of one hour =

    _____

17. **Round** 19.99 to three significant digits. _____
18. The next **prime number** after 13 is _____ .
19. **Square** 17 and **add** 11. _____
20. How many **dozen** are there in 1692?

    _____

Score: _____ /20 _____ %

Day 1

1. Evaluate 2^4. _____
2. $0.2 + 2.8 =$ _____
3. $13 - 0.5 =$ _____
4. $50 \times 0.03 =$ _____
5. $0.5 \div 0.05 =$ _____
6. The **probability** of throwing two sixes when two dice are thrown is

   _____.

7. **Round** 1.05 to one **decimal** place.

   _____

8. Write 0.1% as a **fraction** in its simplest form.

   _____

9. $\frac{1}{3} \times$ _____ $= 10$
10. Rewrite 0.061 as a **percentage**. _____
11. $\sqrt{729} =$ _____
12. Does a **circle** have only 360 axes of symmetry?   **Yes   No**
13. The **formula** to calculate the **area** of a **parallelogram** is

    _____.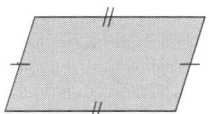

14. Solve for x if $3x = 72 - 6$.

    _____

15. Write the **prime factors** of 21.

    _____

16. **Ten percent** of one hour = _____
17. **Round** 9.99 to three significant digits. _____
18. The next **prime number** after 67 is _____.
19. **Square** 14 and **add** 22. _____
20. How many **dozen** are there in 1704?

    _____

Day 2

1. Evaluate 2^5. _____
2. $2.08 + 8.91 =$ _____
3. $14 - 0.6 =$ _____
4. $50 \times 0.02 =$ _____
5. $0.4 \div 0.04 =$ _____
6. The **probability** of throwing a double when two dice are thrown is

   _____.

7. **Round** 2.45 to one **decimal** place.

   _____

8. Write 0.01% as a **fraction** in its simplest form.

   _____

9. $\frac{1}{3} \times$ _____ $= 12$
10. Rewrite 0.051 as a **percentage**. _____
11. $\sqrt{121} =$ _____
12. Does every **rectangle** have exactly two axes of symmetry?   **Yes   No**
13. The **formula** to calculate the **area** of a **triangle** is

    _____.

14. Draw a **ray** with one endpoint.

    [   ]

15. Write the product of the prime factors of 21.

    _____

16. **Twenty percent** of one hour = _____
17. **Round** 9.98 to two significant digits. _____
18. The next **prime number** after 89 is _____.
19. **Square** 16 and **add** 13. _____
20. How many **dozen** are there in 1716?

    _____

Day 3

1. **Evaluate** 10^{-1}. _____
2. $1.6 + 1.5 =$ _____
3. $3 - 0.05 =$ _____
4. $0.20 \times 0.03 =$ _____
5. $0.3 \div 0.03 =$ _____
6. If $x = -3$, find the value of $2x$.

   _____
7. **Round** 1.009 to one **decimal** place. _____
8. If the **perimeter** of a **rhombus** is 16 in., its side length is

   _____.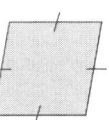
9. $^1/_3 \times$ _____ $= 40$
10. Rewrite 0.062 as a **percentage**. _____
11. $\sqrt{225} =$ _____
12. List the **elements** in common for the **multisets** [1, 3, 5, 7, 9] and [1, 1, 2, 3, 5].

    _____
13. The **formula** to calculate the **surface area** of a **cube** is

    _____.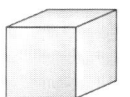
14. The **chance** of drawing a ♠ (spades) card from a deck of cards is

    _____.
15. The symbol ∈ means

    _____.
16. **Fifteen percent** of one hour = _____
17. **Round** 19.98 to three significant digits.

    _____
18. **Square** 19 and **add** 16. _____
19. $\$3 - \$0.5 =$ _____
20. If $y = 12$, find the value of $8y - 3$. _____

Day 4

1. **Evaluate** 10^{-2}. _____
2. $1.7 + 1.6 =$ _____
3. $4 - 0.005 =$ _____
4. $0.20 \times 0.002 =$ _____
5. $0.2 \div 0.02 =$ _____
6. If $x = -3$, find the value of $3x$.

   _____
7. **Round** 1.099 to one **decimal** place.

   _____
8. If the **perimeter** of an **equilateral triangle** is 54 in., its side length is

   _____.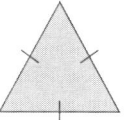
9. $^1/_3 \times$ _____ $= 70$
10. Rewrite 0.063 as a **percentage**. _____
11. $\sqrt{169} =$ _____
12. List the **elements** in common for the **sets** [2, 4, 6, 8, 0] and [2, 3, 5, 7].

    _____
13. The **formula** to calculate the **surface area** of a **cylinder** is

    _____.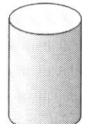
14. The **chance** of drawing two ♥ (hearts) cards in a row without replacing the cards is

    _____.
15. The symbol ⟷ means

    _____

    _____.
16. **Thirty percent** of one hour = _____
17. **Round** 9.95 to one significant digit. _____
18. **Square** 21 and **add** 27. _____
19. $\$4 - \$0.65 =$ _____
20. How many **dozen** are there in 1728?

    _____

Score: ___/20   %   Score: ___/20   %

Week 26

Day 1

1. Evaluate 2^{-4}. _____

2. $20 + 0.01 =$ _____

3. $20 - 0.01 =$ _____

4. $20 \times 0.01 =$ _____

5. $20 \div 0.01 =$ _____

6. If the **perimeter** of an **equilateral triangle** is 36 in., one side's length is _____.

7. **Round** 1.049 to one **decimal** place. _____

8. What 2-D **shape** occurs on the cutting faces when a **cube** is cut through on the diagonal?

_____

9. $\frac{1}{3} \times$ _____ $= 200$

10. Rewrite 0.072 as a **percentage**. _____

11. $\sqrt{324} =$ _____

12. The symbol $\approx$ means _____.

13. The **formula** to calculate the **area** of a **square** is

_____.

14. The **chance** of randomly drawing a ♣ (clubs) face card (jack, queen, king) from a deck is

_____

15. The symbol $\notin$ means

_____

16. What **fraction** of this shape is shaded?

_____

17. **Round** 4.956 to two significant digits. _____

18. The next **prime number** after 83 is _____.

19. **Square** 30 and **add** 22. _____

20. How many **dozen** are there in 1740? _____

Score: /20   %

Day 2

1. Evaluate 2^{-5}. _____

2. $20 + 0.04 =$ _____

3. $20 - 0.04 =$ _____

4. $20 \times 0.04 =$ _____

5. $20 \div 0.04 =$ _____

6. What is the **diameter** of a protractor with a **radius** of 5 in.? _____

5 in.

7. **Round** 1.029 to one **decimal** place. _____

8. What 2-D **shape** occurs on the cutting faces when a **cube** is cut through on the horizontal?

_____

9. $\frac{1}{3} \times$ _____ $= 2$

10. Rewrite 0.077 as a **percentage**. _____

11. $\sqrt{196} =$ _____

12. The symbol $\neq$ means

_____

13. The symbol $\therefore$ means _____.

14. The chance of randomly drawing a card that is not a ♣ (clubs) face card is _____.

15. If the **average** number of the children in a family is 2.3, which type of average is it?

(a) mean   (b) mode   (c) median

16. What **fraction** of this shape is shaded?

_____

17. **Round** 4.90 to one significant digit. _____

18. The next **prime number** after 73 is _____.

19. **Square** 30 and **add** 30^2. _____

20. How many **dozen** are there in 1752? _____

Score: /20   %

Day 3

1. Express as a **fraction**: 12^{-2}. _____

2. $1.8 + 1.9 =$ _____

3. $3 - 2.55 =$ _____

4. $0.20 \times 0.03 =$ _____

5. $0.1 \div 0.01 =$ _____

6. What **number** is halfway between -8 and 2?

   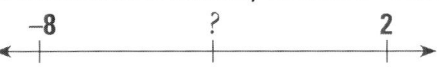

   _____

7. Today's date in **international standard date** notation is ____ / ____ / ____.

8. List the **elements** in common for the **sets** [1, 2, 3, 4, 5] and [2, 4, 6, 8].

   _____

9. If one gallon of gas costs $1.50 and produces 19.75 pounds of CO_2 (carbon dioxide) emissions, how much CO_2 is produced each time I fill my tank at a cost of $60?

   _____

10. Rewrite 0.066 as a **percentage**. _____

11. $50^2 =$ _____

12. $(-64) \div (-32) =$ _____

13. Simplify $6p^2 \times p^3$. _____

14. **Round** 1.1119 to one **decimal** place.

    _____

15. **Rewrite** $120 as a **ratio** of 1 : 5 _____

16. The **chance** of *not* drawing the ace of ♦ (diamonds) from a deck of cards is

    _____ .

17. **Round** 17.95 to three significant digits. _____

18. **Ninety-nine percent** of 400 =

    _____

19. **Square** 200 and **add** 2. _____

20. If $x = 4.5$, find the value of $4x - 6$.

    _____

Day 4

1. Express as a **fraction**: 8^{-2}. _____

2. $1.4 + 1.8 =$ _____

3. $4 - 0.505 =$ _____

4. $0.20 \times 0.002 =$ _____

5. $0.2 \div 0.02 =$ _____

6. What **number** is halfway between -6 and 10?

   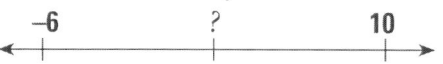

   _____

7. What type of **graph** is this?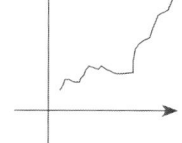

   (a) line graph

   (b) pie graph

   (c) histogram

8. List the **elements** in common for the **sets** [2, 4, 6, 8] and [4, 8, 12, 16].

   _____

9. How many dimes make up $100? _____

10. Rewrite 0.165 as a **percentage**. _____

11. $49 \times 51 =$ _____

12. $(-34) \div (-17) =$ _____

13. Simplify $3z^2 \times 2z^4$. _____

14. **Round** 1.109 to one **decimal** place. _____

15. **Divide** $30 by the **ratio** 1 : 5. _____

16. What is this? $A \bullet\!\!-\!\!\!-\!\!\!-\!\!\bullet B$

    _____

17. **Round** 6.95 to two significant digits. _____

18. **Four hundred percent** of 99 = _____

19. **Square** 100 and **add** 12. _____

20. How many **dozen** are there in 1764?

    _____

Score: _____ /20 _____ %

Score: _____ /20 _____ %

Day 1

1. Evaluate 2^{-4}. _____
2. $20 + 0.03 =$ _____
3. $20 - 0.03 =$ _____
4. $20 \times 0.03 =$ _____
5. $20 \div 0.03 =$ _____
6. If I run at an **average speed** of 6 mph, how far will I have traveled after 15 minutes? _____
7. **Expand** $-3(2 - 2x)$. _____
8. The **variable** "car color" is classified as which type of **data**?
   (a) ordinal   (b) nominal
   (c) continuous   (d) discrete
9. What **number** is halfway between −6 and 2? _____
10. Rewrite 0.565 as a **percentage**. _____
11. Write the time **quarter to seven in the morning** in short form (digital clock format).

    _____
12. Draw a **diagram** to show Set A as a **subset** of Set B.

13. The symbol °C means _____.
14. The **symbol** for "at a particular price each" is _____.
15. What **fraction** of this shape is shaded?

    _____
16. **Forty percent** of one hour = _____
17. **Round** 6.3220 to three significant digits. _____
18. **Square** 300 and **add** 4. _____
19. $3 − $0.50 = _____
20. How many **dozen** are there in 1776? _____

Score: _____ /20 _____ %

Day 2

1. Evaluate 2^{-5}. _____
2. $20 + 0.02 =$ _____
3. $20 - 0.02 =$ _____
4. $20 \times 0.02 =$ _____
5. $20 \div 0.02 =$ _____
6. If I run at an **average speed** of 6 mph, how far will I have traveled after 45 minutes?

   _____
7. **Expand** $-5(3 - 4y)$. _____
8. The **variable** "gender" is classified as which type of **data**?
   (a) ordinal   (b) nominal
   (c) continuous   (d) discrete
9. What **number** is halfway between −4 and 4? _____
10. Rewrite 0.655 as a **percentage**. _____
11. Write the time **twenty minutes to seven in the morning** in short form (digital clock format).

    _____
12. Draw a **diagram** to show sets A and B having no elements in common.

13. The symbol K means _____.
14. Express 1932 in **Roman numerals**. _____
15. What **fraction** of this shape is shaded?

    _____
16. **Sixty percent** of one hour = _____
17. **Round** 6.3220 to two significant digits. _____
18. **Square** 21 and **add** 1. _____
19. $4 − $0.60 = _____
20. How many **dozen** are there in 1788? _____

Score: _____ /20 _____ %

Day 3

1. **Evaluate** 2^{-6}. _____
2. $3.25 + 0.2 =$ _____
3. $3.25 - 0.2 =$ _____
4. $0.20 \times 0.07 =$ _____
5. $0.9 \div 0.09 =$ _____
6. $\sqrt{8}$ is between which two **whole numbers**?
   _____
7. $9 \times 8 - 2 =$ _____
   (Hint: Use PEMDAS.)
8. How many **days** are there in April and May? _____
9. What **number** is halfway between –9 and 7?
   _____
10. Rewrite 0.765 as a **percentage**. _____
11. Draw a **diagram** to show Set A having some elements in common with Set B.

12. Name this **shape**.

    _____
13. Write the time **five minutes past seven in the morning** in short form (digital clock format).
    _____
14. Take 19 from the **sum** of 12 and 13. _____
15. Express the amount MCMLXXXVII in **Arabic** (common) **numerals**. _____
16. **Seventy percent** of one hour = _____
17. **Round** 36.3960 to three significant digits.
    _____
18. The next **prime number** after 19 is _____.
19. **Square** 170 and **add** 22. _____
20. If $x = 16$, find the value of $4x - 6$. _____

Score: /20   %

Day 4

1. **Evaluate** 2^{-7}. _____
2. $4.5 + 0.025 =$ _____
3. $4.5 - 0.025 =$ _____
4. $0.20 \times 0.008 =$ _____
5. $0.8 \div 0.08 =$ _____
6. $\sqrt{13}$ is between which two **whole numbers**?
   _____
7. $9 \times 7 - 3 =$ _____
   (Hint: Use PEMDAS.)
8. How many days are there in September, October, and November? _____
9. What **number** is halfway between –7 and 5?
   _____
10. Rewrite 0.0615 as a **percentage**. _____
11. Complete a **Venn diagram** for the letters in the names "Anna" and "Hannah."

    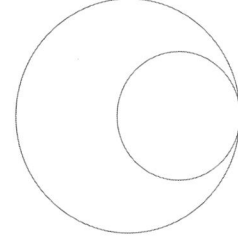

12. Name this **shape**.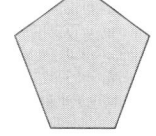

    _____
13. Write the time **five minutes past ten in the morning** in short form (digital clock format).
    _____
14. Add 4 to the **quotient** of 40 and 5. _____
15. Express the amount MCMXCVIII in **Arabic** (common) **numerals**. _____
16. **Eighty percent** of one hour = _____
17. **Round** 6.39800 to two significant digits.
    _____
18. The next **prime number** after 7 is _____.
19. **Square** 15 and **add** 22. _____
20. How many **dozen** are there in 1800? _____

Score: /20   %

Day 1

1. Evaluate 2^{-4}. _____
2. $2.64 + 6.15 =$ _____
3. $3 - 0.5 =$ _____
4. $20 \times 0.03 =$ _____
5. $0.7 \div 0.07 =$ _____
6. Solve for x if $^4/_x = 8$. _____
7. Today's date in **international standard date** notation is ___YYYY_/_MM_/_DD_.
8. $\sqrt{17}$ is between which two **whole numbers**? _____
9. What **number** is halfway between −18 and 26? _____
10. Rewrite 0.047 as a **percentage**. _____
11. The **variable** "temperature" is classified as which type of **data**?

    (a) ordinal   (b) nominal

    (c) continuous (d) discrete
12. Name this **shape**.

    _____

    _____
13. Write **five minutes to three in the afternoon** in short form (digital clock format).

    _____
14. From 8400, take 12. _____
15. Express the amount MCMXC in **Arabic** (common) **numerals**. _____
16. If Kieran earns $78 for six hours of work, what is his hourly **rate of pay**?

    _____
17. **Round** 12.95 to one significant digit.

    _____
18. The next **prime number** after 13 is _____.
19. **Square** 2000 and **add** 2. _____
20. How many **dozen** are there in 1812? _____

Score: _____ /20   _____ %

Day 2

1. Evaluate 2^{-5}. _____
2. $3.25 + 4.03 =$ _____
3. $4 - 0.6 =$ _____
4. $20 \times 0.02 =$ _____
5. $0.6 \div 0.06 =$ _____
6. Solve for x if $^5/_x = 2$. _____
7. How many days are there in December and January?

    _____
8. $\sqrt{86}$ is between which two **whole numbers**?

    _____
9. What **number** is halfway between −28 and 24?

    _____
10. Rewrite 0.015 as a **percentage**. _____
11. The **variable** "crowd size" is classified as which type of **data**?

    (a) ordinal   (b) nominal

    (c) continuous (d) discrete
12. Name this **shape**.

    _____

    _____
13. Write **five minutes to four in the afternoon** in short form (digital clock format).

    _____
14. From 76, take 31. _____
15. Express the amount MCMXCIV in **Arabic** (common) **numerals**. _____
16. If Nicolette earns $56 for seven hours of work, what is her hourly **rate of pay**? _____
17. **Round** 12.9174 to three significant digits.

    _____
18. The next **prime number** after 17 is _____.
19. **Square** 2000 and **add** 20. _____
20. How many **dozen** are there in 1824? _____

Score: _____ /20   _____ %

Day 3

1. Evaluate 3^{-2}. _____
2. 4.03 + 1.07 = _____
3. 3 − 0.05 = _____
4. 0.20 × 0.03 = _____
5. 0.9 ÷ 0.9 = _____
6. Half the **product** of 6 and 8 is _____.
7. Find the **sum** "0.3 plus 0.4 plus 0.9." _____
8. What **number** is halfway between −16 and 12?

   _____
9. $\sqrt{105}$ is between which two **whole numbers**?

   _____
10. Rewrite 0.0665 as a **percentage**. _____
11. **Multiply** 135 by three. _____
12. Name this shape.

    _____

    _____
13. What is the **value** of 2 in 123.456? _____
14. Write the time **five minutes to midday** in short form (digital clock format).

    _____
15. Express the amount MCMXCVI in **Arabic** (common) **numerals**. _____
16. If Robert earns $120 for five hours of work, what is his hourly **rate of pay**?

    _____
17. **Round** 12.90 to two significant digits.

    _____
18. The next **prime number** after five is _____.
19. **Square** 200 and **add** 202. _____
20. If $x = 7$, find the value of $4x − 6$. _____

Day 4

1. Evaluate 3^{-3}. _____
2. 4 + 0.005 = _____
3. 4 − 0.005 = _____
4. 0.20 × 0.2 = _____
5. 0.8 ÷ 0.08 = _____
6. Half the **product** of 11 and 12 is _____.
7. Find the **product** of 0.3 and 5. _____
8. What **number** is halfway between −10 and 8?

   _____
9. $\sqrt{18}$ is between which two **whole numbers**?

   _____
10. Rewrite 0.035 as a **percentage**. _____
11. Complete the **pattern**.

    0, 1, 3, 6, 10, _____, _____
12. Name this **shape**.

    _____

    _____
13. What is the **value** of 3 in 123.456? _____
14. Write the time **ten minutes to midday** in short form (digital clock format).

    _____
15. Express the amount MCMXXXV in **Arabic** (common) **numerals**. _____
16. If Jamal earns $115 for five hours of work, what is his hourly **rate of pay**?

    _____
17. **Round** 12.95 to three significant digits.

    _____
18. The next **prime number** after 7 is _____.
19. **Square** 200 and **add** 2002. _____
20. How many **dozen** are there in 1836?

    _____

Score: _____ /20 _____ %   Score: _____ /20 _____ %

Day 1

1. Evaluate 4^{-4}. _____

2. $3 + 0.51 =$ _____

3. $3 - 0.15 =$ _____

4. $20 \times 0.03 =$ _____

5. $0.7 \div 0.7 =$ _____

6. $(+4) - (-3) - (-9) =$ _____

7. $\sqrt{102}$ is between which two **whole numbers**?

   _____

8. Write the missing numbers in the **pattern**.

   59, 61, 63, _____, _____, 69

9. What **number** is halfway between –5 and 7?

   _____

10. Rewrite 0.025 as a **percentage**. _____

11. What is the **value** of 4 in 123.456?

    _____

12. Name this **shape**.

    _____

    _____

13. What **percentage** of 10 is 8? _____

14. Write the time **ten minutes to eleven in the morning** in short form (digital clock format).

    _____

15. Express the amount MCMLVI in **Arabic** (common) **numerals**. _____

16. If Alexis earns $80 for five hours of work, what is her hourly **rate of pay**?

    _____

17. How many **significant digits** are there in 0.001?

    _____

18. The next **prime number** after 31 is _____.

19. **Square** 20 and add 22^2. _____

20. How many **dozen** are there in 1848?

    _____

Day 2

1. Evaluate 5^{-3}. _____

2. $5.2 + 5.3 =$ _____

3. $4 - 0.16 =$ _____

4. $20 \times 0.02 =$ _____

5. $0.6 \div 0.6 =$ _____

6. $(+ 3) - (-4) - (-8) =$ _____

7. $\sqrt{69}$ is between which two **whole numbers**?

   _____

8. How many days are there in January and February?

   _____

9. What **number** is halfway between –3 and 9?

   _____

10. Rewrite 0.095 as a **percentage**. _____

11. What is the **value** of 5 in 123.456?

    _____

12. Name this **shape**.

    _____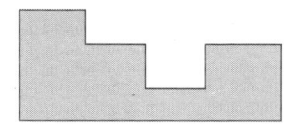

    _____

13. What **percentage** of 10 is 55? _____

14. Write the time **ten minutes to midnight** in short form (digital clock format).

    _____

15. Express the amount MCMLXIII in **Arabic** (common) **numerals**. _____

16. If David earns $95 for five hours of work, what is his hourly **rate of pay**?

    _____

17. How many **significant digits** are there in 0.01?

    _____

18. The next **prime number** after 41 is _____.

19. **Square** 22 and add 22. _____

20. How many **dozen** are there in 1860?

    _____

Score: _____ /20 _____ %   Score: _____ /20 _____ %

Day 3

1. Evaluate 2^{-8}. _____

2. $0.3 + 0.06 =$ _____

3. $8.5 - 0.05 =$ _____

4. $0.20 \times 0.03 =$ _____

5. $0.9 \div 0.03 =$ _____

6. $(+3) - (-2) - (-7) =$ _____

7. $\sqrt{42}$ is between which two **whole numbers**?
   _____

8. How many days are there in July and August?
   _____

9. What **number** is halfway between −11 and 5?
   _____

10. Rewrite 0.065 as a **percentage**. _____

11. Is this network **traversable**?

    Yes   No

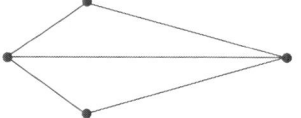

12. Name this **shape**.

    _____

    _____

13. What **percentage** of 10 is 6? _____

14. Write **twenty-five minutes to seven in the evening** in short form (digital clock format).

    _____

15. Express the amount MMVIII in **Arabic** (common) **numerals**. _____

16. If Megan earns $90 for five hours of work, what is her hourly **rate of pay**?

    _____

17. How many **significant digits** are there in 3.14?

    _____

18. The next **prime number** after 101 is _____.

19. **Square** 22 and **add** 20. _____

20. If $x = 5$, find the value of $4x - 6$. _____

Score: _____ /20 _____ %

Day 4

1. Evaluate 2^{-7}. _____

2. $0.66 + 0.33 =$ _____

3. $4.2 - 0.003 =$ _____

4. $0.20 \times 0.22 =$ _____

5. $0.9 \div 0.90 =$ _____

6. $(+3) - (-1) - (-2) =$ _____

7. $\sqrt{39}$ is between which two **whole numbers**?
   _____

8. How many days are there in September and October?
   _____

9. What **number** is halfway between −4 and 8?
   _____

10. Rewrite 0.011 as a **percentage**. _____

11. Find the measure of angle $x°$.

12. Name this **shape**.

    _____

    _____

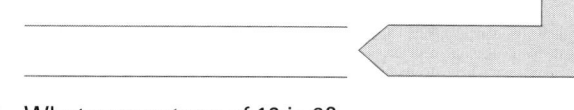

13. What **percentage** of 10 is 9? _____

14. Write **quarter to seven in the evening** in short form (digital clock format). _____

15. Express the amount MCMXCIX in **Arabic** (common) **numerals**. _____

16. If Miroslav earns $95 for five hours of work, what is his hourly **rate of pay**? _____

17. How many **significant digits** are there in 3.141?

    _____

18. The next **prime number** after 11 is _____.

19. **Square** 22 and **add** 12. _____

20. How many **dozen** are there in 1872? _____

Score: _____ /20 _____ %

Day 1

1. Evaluate 4^{-4}. _____

2. $40.4 + 23.8 =$ _____

3. $3 - 0.355 =$ _____

4. $200 \times 0.03 =$ _____

5. $0.6 \div 0.03 =$ _____

6. $(+1) - (-1) - (-1) =$ _____

7. $\sqrt{24}$ is between which two **whole numbers**?

   _____

8. Write the missing numbers in the **pattern**.

   590, 610, 630, _____, _____, 690

9. What **number** is halfway between −12 and 2?

   _____

10. Rewrite 0.045 as a **percentage**. _____

11. Write the time **twenty minutes to nine in the morning** in short form (digital clock format).

    _____

12. Name this **shape**.

    _____

    _____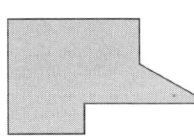

13. What **percentage** of 10 is 2.5? _____

14. Write the time **twenty-five minutes to seven in the morning** in short form (digital clock format).

    _____

15. Express the amount MMV in **Arabic**

    (common) **numerals**. _____

16. If Fiona earns $185 for five hours of work, what is her hourly **rate of pay**?

    _____

17. Round **pi** to one **significant digit**.

    _____

18. The next **prime number** after 41 is _____.

19. **Square** 15 and **add** 22. _____

20. How many **dozen** are there in 1884?

    _____

Score: _____ /20 _____ %

Day 2

1. Evaluate 8^{-3}. _____

2. $6.42 + 2.17 =$ _____

3. $4 - 0.16 =$ _____

4. $20 \times 0.011 =$ _____

5. $0.9 \div 0.03 =$ _____

6. $(+3) - (-3) - (-3) =$ _____

7. $\sqrt{11}$ is between which two **whole numbers**?

   _____

8. Write the missing numbers in the **pattern**.

   0.59, 0.61, 0.63, _____, _____, 0.69

9. What **number** is halfway between −6 and 10?

   _____

10. Rewrite 0.054 as a **percentage**. _____

11. Write the time **quarter to eleven in the morning** in short form (digital clock format).

    _____

12. Name this **shape**.

    _____

    _____

13. What **percentage** of 10 is 3? _____

14. Write the time **twenty-five minutes to ten in the evening** in short form (digital clock format).

    _____

15. Express the amount MMI in **Arabic**

    (common) **numerals**. _____

16. If Evan earns $100 for five hours of work, what is his hourly **rate of pay**?

    _____

17. Round **pi** to two **significant digits**.

    _____

18. The next **prime number** after 61 is _____.

19. **Square** 15 and **add** 25. _____

20. How many **dozen** are there in 1896?

    _____

Score: _____ /20 _____ %

Day 3

1. Evaluate 2^{-8}. _____

2. $4.1 + 0.41 + 0.041 =$ _____

3. $3 - 0.08 =$ _____ 4. $0.20 \times 0.25 =$ _____

5. $9 \div 0.09 =$ _____

6. $(+13) - (+4) - (+8) =$ _____

7. $\sqrt{14}$ is between which two **whole numbers**? _____

8. What is the **value** of 8 in 87,123.456? _____

9. What **number** is halfway between −18 and 16? _____

10. Rewrite 0.032 as a **percentage**. _____

11. Write the time **twenty-seven minutes to seven in the morning** in short form (digital clock format).

_____

12. What is the line that joins the midpoint dots on a **histogram** called?

_____

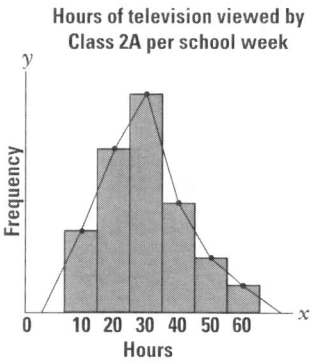

Hours of television viewed by Class 2A per school week

13. Find $^2/_5$ of 405. _____

14. What **percentage** of 10 is 9.5? _____

15. Express the amount MCMXXVI in **Arabic** (common) **numerals**. _____

16. Simplify the **ratio** 0.02 : 0.4. _____

17. **Pi** is most often expressed as how many **significant digits**? _____

18. The next **prime number** after 23 is _____.

19. $202^2 =$ _____

20. If $x = 12$, find the value of $3x - 6$. _____

Day 4

1. Evaluate 2^{-7}. _____

2. $3.2 + 2.3 + 0.23 =$ _____

3. $4 - 0.015 =$ _____

4. $0.20 \times 0.025 =$ _____

5. $8 \div 0.08 =$ _____

6. $(+3) - (+4) - (-8) =$ _____

7. $\sqrt{15}$ is between which two **whole numbers**?

_____

8. What is the **value** of 8 in 123.468?

_____

9. What **number** is halfway between −16 and 14?

_____

10. Rewrite 0.016 as a **percentage**. _____

11. Write the time **ten minutes to seven in the morning** in short form (digital clock format).

_____

12. A bar graph's bars can be horizontal or vertical.

 True   False

13. Find $^3/_5$ of 405. _____

14. What **percentage** of 10 is $8^1/_2$? _____

15. Express the amount MMIV in **Arabic** (common) **numerals**. _____

16. If Adelaide earns $85 for five hours of work, what is her hourly **rate of pay**?

_____

17. How many **significant digits** are there in 0.125? _____

18. The next **prime number** after 113 is _____.

19. **Square** 19 and add 2^2. _____

20. How many **dozen** are there in 1908?

_____

| Score: | /20 | % | Score: | /20 | % |

Day 1

1. **Evaluate** 2^{-4}. _____
2. $0.55 + 0.51 + 0.1 =$ _____
3. $3 - 0.2 =$ _____
4. $20 \times 0.07 =$ _____
5. $7 \div 0.07 =$ _____
6. $(+3) - (+2) - (+8) =$ _____
7. $0.25^2 =$ _____
8. What is the **value** of 2 in 7123.456?

   _____
9. What **number** is halfway between −14 and 28?

   _____
10. Rewrite 0.068 as a **percentage**. _____
11. What is the **value** of 6 in 123.456?

   _____
12. Which type of **graph** is usually used to show **data** over time?

   _____
13. Find the value of $(2^1/_2)^2$. _____
14. What **percentage** of 10 is 2.8? _____
15. Write the time **twenty minutes to seven in the morning** in short form (digital clock format).

   _____
16. Simplify the **ratio** 0.07 : 0.42.
    (Hint: Convert to whole numbers first.)

   _____
17. Write **pi** to two decimal places. _____
18. The **ratio** of two siblings' ages is 1 : 5. If the sum of their ages is 6, how old are they each?

   Younger sibling = _____

   Older sibling = _____
19. **Square** 20 and **add** 29. _____
20. How many **dozen** are there in 1920?

   _____

Day 2

1. **Evaluate** 2^{-5}. _____
2. $0.04 + 0.44 + 0.4 =$ _____
3. $4 - 0.4 =$ _____
4. $20 \times 0.04 =$ _____
5. $6 \div 0.06 =$ _____
6. $(+3) + (-4) + (-8) =$ _____
7. $20^2 =$ _____
8. What is the **value** of 7 in 7123.456?

   _____
9. What **number** is halfway between −15 and 13?

   _____
10. Rewrite 0.067 as a **percentage**. _____
11. What is the **value** of 1 in 123.456?

   _____
12. Which type of **graph** is usually used to show **parts** of a **whole**?

   _____
13. Find the value of $(3^1/_2)^2$. _____
14. What **percentage** of 10 is 2? _____
15. Write the time **twenty minutes to six in the morning** in short form (digital clock format).

   _____
16. If Eloise earns $80 for five hours of work, what is her hourly **rate of pay**?

   _____
17. **Round** π to the nearest **whole number**. _____
18. The **ratio** of two siblings' ages is 1 : 5. If the sum of their ages is 12, how old are they each?

   Younger sibling = _____

   Older sibling = _____
19. **Square** 20 and **add** 22.5. _____
20. How many **dozen** are there in 1932?

   _____

Score: /20   %   Score: /20   %

Day 3

1. Evaluate 6^{-2}. _____
2. $^1/_9 + ^1/_3 =$ _____
3. $3 - 0.095 =$ _____
4. $0.20 \times 0.03 =$ _____
5. $4 \div 0.04 =$ _____
6. $(+3) - (+3) - (+3) =$ _____
7. Today's date in **international standard date** notation is _____/_____/_____.
8. $11^2 =$ _____
9. What **number** is halfway between −10 and 2? _____
10. Rewrite 0.076 as a **percentage**. _____
11. Write the time **quarter to one in the morning** in short form (digital clock format). _____
12. What is the **value** of 2 in 894.321? _____
13. What **percentage** of 10 is 5? _____
14. $16 \div ^1/_3 =$ _____.
15. Express the amount MMLVI in **Arabic** (common) **numerals**. _____
16. Simplify the **ratio** 0.11 : 0.44. _____
17. 3.141 is π to how many **significant digits**? _____
18. The **ratio** of two siblings' ages is 3 : 4. If the sum of their ages is seven, how old are they each?

    Younger sibling = _____

    Older sibling = _____
19. **Square** 20 and **add** 2.2. _____
20. If $x = 6$, find the value of $4x - 6$. _____

Day 4

1. Evaluate 7^{-2}. _____
2. $^1/_6 + ^1/_3 =$ _____
3. $4 - 0.009 =$ _____
4. $0.20 \times 0.001 =$ _____
5. $3 \div 0.03 =$ _____
6. $(+3) - (+4) + (-8) =$ _____
7. Which type of **graph** is only used to show **quantity** of **frequency**?

    _____
8. $0.01^2 =$ _____
9. What number is halfway between −8 and 6?

    _____
10. Rewrite 0.096 as a **percentage**. _____
11. Write the time **quarter to seven in the evening** in short form (digital clock format).

    _____
12. What is the **place value** of 4 in 987.471?

    _____
13. What **percentage** of 10 is $7^1/_2$? _____
14. $9 \div ^1/_3 =$ _____.
15. Express the amount MMXX in **Arabic** (common) **numerals**. _____
16. If Aldo earns $75 for five hours of work, what is his hourly **rate of pay**?

    _____
17. 3.141 is π to how many **decimal** places?

    _____
18. The **ratio** of two siblings' ages is 5 : 6. If the sum of their ages is 11, how old are they each?

    Younger sibling = _____

    Older sibling = _____
19. **Square** 20 and **add** 0.22. _____
20. How many **dozen** are there in 1944?

    _____

Score: _____ /20 _____ %

Score: _____ /20 _____ %

Week 32

Day 1

1. Evaluate 8^{-2}. _____

2. 2.4 + 1.09 = _____

3. 3 − 0.7 = _____

4. 20 × 0.03 = _____

5. 2 ÷ 0.02 = _____

6. If gold **costs** $800 per ounce, how much would a two-ounce gold ingot be worth?

    _____

7. What amount of carpet is needed for a rectangular room measuring 12 yards by 8 yards? _____

8. 0.3^2 = _____

9. What **number** is halfway between −28 and 22?

    _____

10. Rewrite 0.0875 as a **percentage**. _____

11. Write the time **quarter to seven in the morning** in short form (digital clock format).

    _____

12. Which type of **display of data** does not have gaps between its columns?

    (a) line graph
    (b) bar graph
    (c) histogram

13. What **percentage** of 10 is 4.5? _____

14. 12 ÷ $^{1}/_{2}$ = _____

15. Express the amount MMXL in **Arabic** (common) **numerals**. _____

16. Simplify the **ratio** 0.02 : 0.46. _____

17. 3.1415 is _____ rounded to four **decimal** places.

18. The **ratio** of two siblings' ages is 3 : 4. If the sum of their ages is 14, how old are they each?

    Younger sibling = _____

    Older sibling = _____

19. **Square** 20 and **add** 1.5. _____

20. How many **dozen** are there in 1956? _____

Day 2

1. Evaluate 9^{-2}. _____

2. 2.4 + 0.08 = _____

3. 4 − 0.3 = _____   4. 20 × 0.05 = _____

5. 1 ÷ 0.01 = _____

6. If gold **costs** $800 per ounce, how much is 105 pounds worth?

    _____

7. What amount of carpet is needed for a rectangular room measuring 12 yards by 9 yards?

    _____

8. 2.2^2 = _____

9. What **number** is halfway between −18 and 2?

    _____

10. Rewrite 0.0865 as a **percentage**. _____

11. Write the time **quarter to twelve in the morning** in short form (digital clock format).

    _____

12. A **frequency polygon** is part of what type of display of data?

    _____

13. What **percentage** of 10 is 6.5? _____

14. 20 ÷ $^{1}/_{2}$ = _____

15. Express the amount MMXIX in **Arabic** (common) **numerals**. _____

16. If Cato earns $65 for five hours of work, what is his hourly **rate of pay**? _____

17. The **number** 1.618 is also known as the

    g_____ r_____.

18. The **ratio** of two siblings' ages is 3 : 5. If the sum of their ages is 16, how old are they each?

    Younger sibling = _____

    Older sibling = _____

19. **Square** 15 and **add** 2.5. _____

20. How many **dozen** are there in 1968? _____

Score: _____ /20 _____ %   Score: _____ /20 _____ %

Day 3

1. Evaluate 11^{-2}. _____
2. $0.6 + 0.25 =$ _____
3. $3 - 0.05 =$ _____
4. $0.20 \times 0.03 =$ _____
5. $90 \div 0.09 =$ _____
6. $5 \times \sqrt{2 + 7} =$ _____
7. Today's date in **international standard date** notation is ⎯YYYY⎯/⎯MM⎯/⎯DD⎯.
8. $5.5^2 =$ _____
9. The **sum** of two numbers is 5. If one of the numbers is 8, what is the other number?

   _____
10. Rewrite 0.085 as a **percentage**. _____
11. What **percentage** of 10 is 1? _____
12. What is a **frequency polygon**?

   _____

   _____
13. If Carl traveled at a speed 80 km/h for three hours, how far did he travel?

   _____
14. $12 \div \frac{1}{4} =$ _____
15. Express the amount MMXVIII in **Arabic** (common) **numerals**. _____
16. Simplify the **ratio** 0.03 : 0.9. _____
17. This type of **isosceles triangle** is called a

   g_____
   triangle.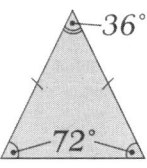
18. The next **prime number** after 17 is _____.
19. **Square** 12 and **add** 6.4. _____
20. If $x = 5$, find the value of $4x - 6$. _____

Day 4

1. Evaluate 12^{-2}. _____
2. $0.231 + 0.123 =$ _____
3. $4 - 0.005 =$ _____
4. $0.20 \times 0.002 =$ _____
5. $80 \div 0.08 =$ _____
6. $4 \times \sqrt{24 + 2 \times 60} =$ _____
7. What amount of carpet is needed for a rectangular room measuring 12 feet by 11 feet?

   _____
8. $5.1^2 =$ _____
9. The **sum** of two numbers is 3. If one of the numbers is 7, what is the other number?

   _____
10. Rewrite 0.086 as a **percentage**. _____
11. What **percentage** of 10 is $1\frac{1}{2}$? _____
12. The middle value or the average of the two middle values in an ordered data set is the

   _____.
13. Write Louis XVIII using **Arabic** (common) **numerals**. _____
14. $13 \div \frac{1}{4} =$ _____
15. Express the amount MMXV in **Arabic** (common) **numerals**. _____
16. If Clancy earns $60 for five hours of work, what is his hourly **rate of pay**?

   _____
17. The Parthenon's proportions approximate the golden **ratio**. State the **ratio** to two **decimal** places.

   _____
18. The next **prime number** after 19 is _____.
19. **Square** 13 and **add** 2.2. _____
20. How many **dozen** are there in 1980? _____

Score: _____ /20 _____ %   Score: _____ /20 _____ %

Day 1

1. **Evaluate** 5^{-2}. _____
2. $2.11 + 3.67 =$ _____
3. $3 - 0.25 =$ _____
4. $20 \times 0.13 =$ _____
5. $70 \div 0.07 =$ _____
6. $(1/2)^{-2} =$ _____
7. $5.2^2 =$ _____
8. If Nellie **saves** $5 per week, how much does she save each year?

    _____
9. The **sum** of two numbers is 6. If one of the numbers is 9, what is the other number?

    _____
10. Rewrite 0.089 as a **percentage**. _____
11. $\sqrt{13^2 - 5^2} =$ _____
12. Calculate the **angle measure** of $y°$.

    _____
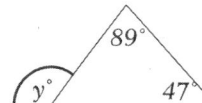
13. A **circle** has which type of symmetry?

    _____
14. Write George VI using **Arabic** (common) **numerals**. _____

15. Express the amount MMIX in **Arabic** (common) **numerals**. _____
16. Simplify the **ratio** 0.02 : 0.6 _____
17. The **metric prefix** for 1 million is

    _____.
18. The next **prime number** after 11 is _____.
19. **Square** 17 and **add** 2.2. _____
20. How many **dozen** are there in 1992?

    _____

Score: ____ /20   ____ %

Day 2

1. **Evaluate** 6^{-3}. _____
2. $0.55 + 0.44 =$ _____
3. $4 - 0.6 =$ _____
4. $20 \times 0.02 =$ _____
5. $60 \div 0.06 =$ _____
6. $(1/4)^2 =$ _____
7. $5.3^2 =$ _____
8. If Sara **saves** $7.50 per week, how much does she save each year?_____
9. The **sum** of two numbers is 4. If one of the numbers is 8, what is the other number?

    _____
10. Rewrite 0.0825 as a **percentage**. _____
11. $\sqrt{10^2 - 6^2} =$ _____
12. Calculate the **angle measure** of $x°$.

    _____
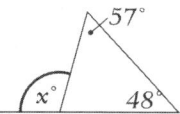
13. How many lines of symmetry does a **circle** have?

    _____
14. Write Edward VIII using **Arabic** (common) **numerals**. _____
15. Express the amount MMIX in **Arabic** (common) **numerals**. _____
16. If Banjo earns $55 for five hours of work, what is his hourly **rate of pay**?

    _____
17. The **ratio** of two siblings' ages is 4 : 5. If the sum of their ages is nine, how old are they each?

    Younger sibling = _____

    Older sibling = _____
18. The next **prime number** after 13 is _____.
19. **Square** 13 and **add** 3.5. _____
20. How many **dozen** are there in 2004? _____

Score: ____ /20   ____ %

Day 3

1. Evaluate 7^{-3}. _____

2. $12.98 + 13 =$ _____

3. $3 - 0.05 =$ _____ 4. $0.20 \times 0.03 =$ _____

5. $4 \div 0.04 =$ _____

6. Solve for x if $\dfrac{3x + 6}{3} = 24$. _____

7. $5.4^2 =$ _____

8. If Julia **saves** $12 per week, how much does she save each year? _____

9. The **sum** of two numbers is 7. If one of the numbers is 8, what is the other number?

    _____

10. Rewrite 0.069 as a **percentage**. _____

11. Evaluate 10^{-1}. _____

12. Calculate the **size** of $w°$.

    _____

13. Where might patterns of **triangular numbers**, **tetrahedral numbers**, **natural numbers**, and **Fibonacci numbers** be found?

    _____

    _____

14. Write Henry VIII using **Arabic** (common) **numerals**. _____

15. Express the amount MMXXIII in **Arabic** (common) **numerals**. _____

16. Simplify the **ratio** 0.02 : 0.4 _____

17. The **ratio** of two siblings' ages is 4 : 5. If the sum of their ages is 36, how old are they each?

    Younger sibling = _____

    Older sibling = _____

18. What is an **irrational number**?

    _____

    _____

19. **Square** 10 and **subtract** 22. _____

20. If $x = 2$, find the value of $4x - 6$. _____

Day 4

1. Evaluate 6^{-3}. _____

2. 130 cm $+ 1$ m $=$ _____

3. $4 - 0.005 =$ _____

4. $0.20 \times 0.002 =$ _____

5. $3 \div 0.03 =$ _____

6. Solve for x if $x - 4 = 15$. _____

7. $5.5^2 =$ _____

8. If Freya **saves** $16 per week, how much does she save each year? _____

9. The **sum** of two numbers is 2. If one of the numbers is 8, what is the other number?

    _____

10. Rewrite 0.079 as a **percentage**. _____

11. Evaluate 3^{-1}. _____

12. Calculate the **size** of $z°$.

    _____

13. What is mathematically remarkable about a chambered nautilus?

    _____

    _____

14. Write William IV using **Arabic** (common) **numerals**. _____

15. Express the amount MMXII in **Arabic** (common) **numerals**. _____

16. If Matilda earns $50 for five hours of work, what is her hourly **rate of pay**?

    _____

17. The **ratio** of two siblings' ages is 3 : 4. If the sum of their ages is 35, how old are they each?

    Younger sibling = _____

    Older sibling = _____

18. Are **irrational numbers** integers? Yes No

19. **Square** 10 and **subtract** 25. _____

20. How many **dozen** are there in 2016? _____

Week 34

Day 1

1. Evaluate 2^{-4}. _____

2. $6.2 + 5.8 =$ _____   3. $3 - 0.5 =$ _____

4. $20 \times 0.03 =$ _____

5. $4 \div 0.04 =$ _____

6. Solve for x if $x/_2 = 11$. _____

7. $5.6^2 =$ _____

8. If Romeo and Juliet **save** $300 per week, how much do they save each year?

   _____

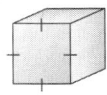

9. The **surface area** of this **cube** is _____.

   7 in.

10. Draw a **concave parabola**.

11. If my bus arrived 35 minutes late and was due at 7:25 a.m., at what time did it arrive?

    _____

12. Calculate the **angle measure** of $y°$.

    _____

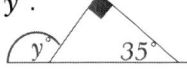

    $y°$ $35°$

13. What **percentage** of 10 is 80? _____

14. The Battle of Hastings took place in MLXVI. What year was this?

    _____

15. Express the amount MMXVI in **Arabic (common) numerals**. _____

16. Simplify the **ratio** 0.02 : 0.1 _____

17. The **ratio** of two siblings' ages is 4 : 5. If the sum of their ages is 27, how old are they each?

    Younger sibling = _____

    Older sibling = _____

18. What is the maximum number of odd vertices needed for a **network** to be **traversable**?

    _____

19. **Square** 11 and **add** 2.2. _____

20. How many **dozen** are there in 2028? _____

Day 2

1. Evaluate 2^{-10}. _____

2. $6.31 + 7.2 =$ _____

3. $4 - 0.6 =$ _____   4. $20 \times 0.02 =$ _____

5. $3 \div 0.03 =$ _____

6. Solve for x if $x/_4 = 9$. _____

7. $5.7^2 =$ _____

8. If Teal **saves** $150 per week, how much does she save each year?

   _____

9. The **volume** of this **cube** is _____.

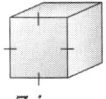

   2 in.

10. How much **compound interest** is due on $2000 at 7% for two years?

    _____

11. If my bus arrived 15 minutes late and was due at 7:40 a.m., at what time did it arrive?

    _____

12. Calculate the **angle measure** of $x°$.

    _____

    $75°$ $x°$ $60°$

13. What **percentage** of 10 is 20? _____

14. Richard the Lionheart reigned from MCLXXXIX to MCXCIX. How many years did he reign?

    _____

15. Express the amount MMXXVIII in **Arabic (common) numerals**. _____

16. If Anne earns $45 for five hours of work, what is her hourly **rate of pay**? _____

17. The **ratio** of two siblings' ages is 3 : 4. If the sum of their ages is 21, how old are they each?

    Younger sibling = _____

    Older sibling = _____

18. Is this network **traversable?** Yes   No

19. **Square** 120 and **add** 33. _____

20. How many **dozen** are there in 2040? _____

Score: ___/20 ___%   Score: ___/20 ___%

Day 3

1. Evaluate 2^{-11}. _____

2. $0.1 + 0.2 + 0.3 + 0.4 =$ _____
    (Hint: Add in pairs.)

3. $3 - 0.05 =$ _____

4. $0.40 \times 0.3 =$ _____

5. $2 \div 0.02 =$ _____

6. The **surface area** of this **cube** is _____ .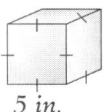
    5 in.

7. $5.8^2 =$ _____

8. If Francesca stops **spending** $3 on a cup of coffee each weekday, how much will she **save** in a year?

    _____

9. How many **quadrants** are there in a **circle**?

    _____

10. Rewrite 0.0699 as a **percentage**. _____

11. If my bus arrived 50 minutes late and was due at 7:55 a.m., at what time did it arrive?

    _____

12. Calculate the **angle measure** of $a°$.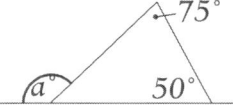

    _____

13. $12 \div \frac{1}{3} =$ _____

14. Express Elizabeth I's reign from 1558 to 1603 in **Roman numerals**.

    _____

15. Express the amount MMXXXII in **Arabic** (common) **numerals**. _____

16. Simplify the **ratio** 0.02 : 0.8. _____

17. Simplify the **ratio** three days : three weeks. _____

18. The next **prime number** after 89 is _____ .

19. **Square** 20 and **add** 22. _____

20. If $x = 11$, find the value of $4x - 6$. _____

Day 4

1. Evaluate 2^{-12}. _____

2. **Sum** the numbers 0.1 to 1.0. _____
    (Add only numbers to one decimal point.)

3. $4 - 0.005 =$ _____

4. $0.10 \times 0.032 =$ _____

5. $1 \div 0.01 =$ _____

6. The **surface area** of this **cube** is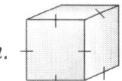

    _____ .
    6 in.

7. $5.9^2 =$ _____

8. Louis stops buying a daily paper to repay a debt. If the paper **costs** $1.50, how soon will it be before his $300 debt is paid?

    _____

9. How many **faces** are there on a **cone**? _____

10. Rewrite 0.0799 as a **percentage**. _____

11. If my bus arrived 25 minutes late and was due at 7:05 a.m., at what time did it arrive?

    _____

12. Calculate the **angle measure** of $b°$.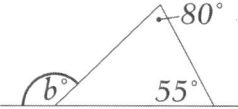

    _____

13. $6 \div \frac{1}{3} =$ _____

14. In C CE, the Roman Empire was at its greatest size. Express the year in **Arabic numerals**.

    _____

15. Express the amount MMXXX in **Arabic** (common) **numerals**. _____

16. If Anne earns $40 for five hours of work, what is her hourly **rate of pay**?

    _____

17. Simplify the **ratio** of 14 days : five weeks. _____

18. The next **prime number** after 97 is _____ .

19. **Square** 2 and **add** 22. _____

20. How many **dozen** are there in 2052? _____

Day 1

1. Evaluate 2^{-2}. _____
2. $7.06 + 2.994 =$ _____
3. $3 - 0.5 =$ _____
4. $20 \times 0.03 =$ _____
5. $80 \div 0.08 =$ _____
6. Is a **circle** a **polygon?**   Yes   No
7. $2.1^2 =$ _____
8. If Michaela **saves** $32 per week, how much is this per year?

   _____

9. What is the angle sum of any **quadrilateral?** _____
10. If one face of a Rubik's Cube® puzzle is three blocks tall, three blocks wide and three blocks long, and each square block is 1.2 cm long, what is the approximate **volume** of a **whole cube?**

    _____

11. Is the **slope** of **line** k positive or negative?

    (a) positive   (b) negative

    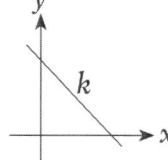

12. If my bus arrived 55 minutes late and was due at 7:55 a.m., at what time did it arrive?

    _____

13. What **percentage** of 100 is 8? _____
14. $12,000 \div \frac{1}{2} =$ _____
15. Express the amount MMXLII in **Arabic** (common) **numerals.** _____
16. Simplify the **ratio** 0.02 : 0.6. _____
17. Simplify the **ratio** six days : three weeks. _____
18. The next **prime number** after 61 is _____.
19. **Square** 120 and **add** 22. _____
20. How many **dozen** are there in 2064?

    _____

Day 2

1. Evaluate 3^{-2}. _____
2. $6.51 + 3.872 =$ _____
3. $4 - 0.6 =$ _____
4. $20 \times 0.02 =$ _____
5. $70 \div 0.07 =$ _____
6. Is a **sphere** a **polyhedron?**   Yes   No
7. $2.2^2 =$ _____
8. If Ellie **saves** $33 per week, how much is this per year?

   _____

9. What is the angle sum of a **pentagon?** _____
10. Calculate the **angle measure** $b°$. (Drawing is not to scale.)

    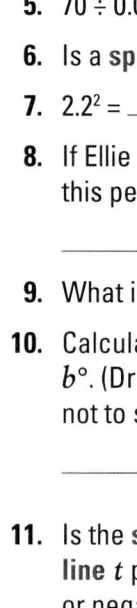

    _____

11. Is the **slope** of **line** t positive or negative?

    (a) positive   (b) negative

    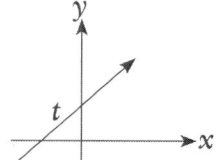

12. If my bus arrived 55 minutes late and was due at 8:10 a.m., at what time did it arrive?

    _____

13. What **percentage** of 100 is 28? _____
14. $29 \div \frac{1}{2} =$ _____
15. Express the amount MMXLIV in **Arabic** (common) **numerals.** _____
16. If Aaron earns $42.50 for five hours of work, what is his hourly **rate of pay?**

    _____

17. Simplify the **ratio** four days : eight weeks. _____
18. The next **prime number** after 67 is _____.
19. **Square** 220 and **add** 22. _____
20. How many **dozen** are there in 2076?

    _____

Score: _____ /20 _____ %   Score: _____ /20 _____ %

Day 3

1. Evaluate 2^{-3}. _____
2. $3.2 + 5.6 =$ _____
3. $3 - 0.05 =$ _____
4. $0.20 \times 0.03 =$ _____
5. $60 \div 0.06 =$ _____
6. The measures of **supplementary angles** sum to _____.
7. $5.5^2 = 30.5$ **Correct   Incorrect**
8. If Mika **saves** $42 per week, how much is this per year? _____
9. Name a figure that has an **angle sum** of 360°. _____
10. If one face of a Rubik's Cube® puzzle is three blocks tall, three blocks wide, and three blocks long, and each square block is 1.2 cm long, what is the **surface area** of a **whole cube**? _____
11. What is a **polygon**? _____ _____
12. Which of these is **not** an abbreviation of a test for **congruent triangles**?
    (a) SSS   (b) SAS   (c) SSA
    (d) ASA   (e) HL
13. What **percentage** of 100 is 0.8? _____
14. $12 \div \frac{1}{5} =$ _____
15. Express the amount MMXLVI in **Arabic** (common) **numerals**. _____
16. Simplify the **ratio** 0.02 : 0.42. _____
17. Simplify the **ratio** of five days : ten weeks. _____
18. The **ratio** of two siblings' ages is 4 : 5. If the sum of their ages is 18, how old are they each?
    Younger sibling = _____
    Older sibling = _____
19. **Square** 210 and **add** 2. _____
20. If $x = 2$, find the value of $4x - 6$. _____

Score: _____ /20 _____ %

Day 4

1. Evaluate 3^{-3}. _____
2. $2.2 + 6.6 =$ _____
3. $4 - 0.005 =$ _____
4. $0.20 \times 0.002 =$ _____
5. $90 \div 0.03 =$ _____
6. Write **Euler's formula** for the surfaces of **polyhedra** (concerning vertices, edges, and faces). _____
7. $\sqrt[3]{8} =$ _____
8. If Henry saves $44 per week, how much is this per year? _____
9. How many degrees are there in a **semicircle**? _____

   90°
10. What is the **capacity** of a shipping container measuring 6.5 ft × 3.2 ft × 2.8 ft? _____
11. What is a **polyhedron**? _____ _____
12. These two **triangles** are:
    (a) congruent.
    (b) similar.

    3 in.   30 in.
13. What **percentage** of 100 is 1? _____
14. $10 \div \frac{1}{5} =$ _____
15. Express the amount MML in **Arabic** (common) **numerals**. _____
16. If Ramondo earns $47.50 for five hours of work, what is his hourly **rate of pay**? _____
17. Simplify the **ratio** of two days : two weeks. _____
18. The **ratio** of two siblings' ages is 4 : 7. If the sum of their ages is 22, how old are they each?
    Younger sibling = _____
    Older sibling = _____
19. **Square** 201 and **add** 2.9. _____
20. How many **dozen** are there in 2088? _____

Score: _____ /20 _____ %

Day 1

1. Evaluate 4^{-4}. _____

2. $1.33 + 0.89 =$ _____

3. $3 - 0.5 =$ _____

4. $20 \times 0.03 =$ _____

5. $80 \div 0.02 =$ _____

6. What is the **angle measure** of a **straight line**? _____

7. $\sqrt[3]{64} =$ _____

8. If Andy **saves** $43 per week, how much is this per year?

   _____

9. CXX + CDLII = _____

10. How many 500 m² house lots are **equivalent** in size to a 2000 m² field?

    _____

11. Is this network **traversable**?

    Yes   No

    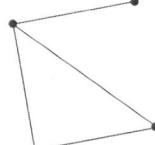

12. If my bus arrived 40 minutes late and was due at 7:45 a.m., at what time did it arrive?

    _____

13. What **percentage** of 1000 is 800? _____

14. $4 \div \frac{1}{3} =$ _____

15. Express the amount MMLX in **Arabic** (common) **numerals**. _____

16. Simplify the **ratio** 0.02 : 0.04. _____

17. Simplify the **ratio** eight days : four weeks.

    _____

18. The next **prime number** after 47 is _____ .

19. **Square** 202 and **add** 1. _____

20. How many **dozen** are there in 2100?

    _____

Day 2

1. Evaluate 4^{-3}. _____

2. $3.33 + 1.67 =$ _____

3. $4 - 0.6 =$ _____

4. $20 \times 0.02 =$ _____

5. $80 \div 0.04 =$ _____

6. What do the measures of two **complementary angles** sum to? _____

7. $\sqrt[3]{125} =$ _____

8. If Pat **saves** $46 per week, how much is this per year?

   _____

9. XML + D = _____

10. If a shipping container measures 6.5 yd × 3.2 yd × 2.8 yd, what is its **surface area**?

    _____

11. Is this network **traversable**?

    Yes   No

    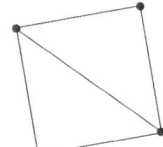

12. If my bus arrived 55 minutes late and was due at 8:05 a.m., at what time did it arrive?

    _____

13. What **percentage** of 1000 is 80? _____

14. $3 \div \frac{1}{4} =$ _____

15. Express the amount MMLXX in **Arabic** (common) **numerals**. _____

16. The **ratio** of two siblings' ages is 4 : 3. If the sum of their ages is 14, how old are they each?

    Older sibling = _____

    Younger sibling = _____

17. Simplify the **ratio** four days : eight weeks. _____

18. The next **prime number** after 53 is _____ .

19. **Square** 202 and **add** 0.2. _____

20. How many **dozen** are there in 2112?

    _____

Score: /20   %   **Score:** /20   %

Day 3

1. Evaluate 2^3. _____
2. $5.23 + 1.87 =$ _____
3. $3 - 0.05 =$ _____
4. $0.20 \times 0.03 =$ _____
5. $60 \div 0.03 =$ _____
6. Write all the **prime numbers** between 10 and 20.

   _____
7. Write today's date in **international standard notation**. YYYY / MM / DD _____ / _____ / _____
8. If Mickie **saves** $48 per week, how much is this per year?

   _____
9. Express the **Roman numerals** CDL in **Arabic** (common) **numerals**. _____
10. Rewrite 0.0899 as a **percentage**. _____
11. Write all of the **factors** of 30.

    _____
12. If my bus arrived 50 minutes late and was due at 9:45 a.m., at what time did it arrive?

    _____
13. What **percentage** of 1000 is 8? _____
14. Find the **product** of $^1/_2 \times ^3/_4$. _____
15. Express the amount MMLXXX in **Arabic** (common) **numerals**. _____
16. Simplify the **ratio** 0.2 : 0.4. _____
17. What amount of carpet is needed to cover a room 12 yards long by 4 yards wide?

    _____
18. The next **prime number** after 101 is _____.
19. Write $^{27}/_5$ as a **mixed number**. _____
20. If $x = 7$, find the value of $4x - 6$. _____

Day 4

1. Evaluate 260^4. _____
2. $0.67 + 0.53 =$ _____
3. $4 - 0.005 =$ _____
4. $0.20 \times 0.002 =$ _____
5. $90 \div 0.45 =$ _____
6. Write all the **prime numbers** between 20 and 30.

   _____
7. Home water usage is usually **measured** in what **unit**?_____.
8. If Pajeet **saves** $47 per week, how much is this per year?

   _____
9. Write the **Roman numerals** CD in **Arabic** (common) **numerals**. _____
10. Rewrite 0.0999 as a **percentage**. _____
11. Write all of the **factors** of 31.

    _____
12. If my bus arrived 15 minutes late and was due at 8:55 a.m., at what time did it arrive?

    _____
13. What **percentage** of 1000 is 10? _____
14. Simplify $^8/_{10}$. _____
15. Express the amount MMXC in **Arabic** (common) **numerals**. _____
16. The **ratio** of two siblings' ages is 5 : 2. If the sum of their ages is 21, how old are they each?

    Older sibling = _____

    Younger sibling = _____
17. What amount of carpet is needed to cover a room 12 feet long by 5 feet wide?

    _____
18. The next **prime number** after 103 is _____.
19. The next **prime number** after 11 is _____.
20. Will the year 4000 be a **leap year**?   Yes   No

Score: _____ /20 _____ %   Score: _____ /20 _____ %

Day 1	Day 2

Day 1

1. **Evaluate** 2^4. _____
2. zero point one one + zero point two = _____
3. $3 - 0.5 =$ _____
4. $20 \times 0.03 =$ _____
5. $70 \div 0.35 =$ _____
6. IX + IV = _____
7. Solve for y: $2y - 3 = 7$. _____
8. If Fred **saves** $25 per week, how much is this per year? _____
9. What does $x > 2$ mean? _____
   _____
10. What **volume** of water would fill an Olympic-size pool? (50 m × 22 m base, with a depth of one meter at one end and two meters at the other)
   _____
11. Is this network **traversable**?
   Yes   No

12. If Shape A is the same shape but **smaller** than Shape B, they are:
   (a) congruent.   (b) similar.
13. What **percentage** of 1000 is 20? _____
14. Simplify $^{32}/_{40}$. _____
15. Express the amount MMC in **Arabic** (common) **numerals**. _____
16. Simplify the **ratio** 0.02 : 0.2. _____
17. Simplify the **ratio** three days : 30 weeks. _____
18. If my bus arrived 45 minutes late and was due at 9:25 a.m., at what time did it arrive?
   _____
19. The next **prime number** after 13 is _____.
20. What is the exact length of a **solar year**?
   _____ days, _____ hours, _____ minutes, and _____ seconds

Day 2

1. **Evaluate** 2^5. _____
2. zero point one two + zero point two one =
   _____
3. $4 - 0.6 =$ _____
4. $20 \times 0.02 =$ _____
5. $77 \div 0.70 =$ _____
6. XC + XIV = _____
7. Solve for y: $2y + 7 = 3$. _____
8. If George **saves** $40 per week, how much is this per year?
   _____
9. What does $x < 2$ mean? _____
   _____
10. **One thousand liters** is equal to what unit of volume? _____
11. Is this network **traversable**?
   Yes   No
   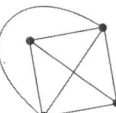
12. If two shapes are **identical** in size and shape, they are:
   (a) congruent.   (b) similar.
13. What **percentage** of 1000 is 3? _____
14. Simplify $^{16}/_{20}$. _____
15. What year is MMCX? _____
16. 90% of one hour is _____
17. Simplify the **ratio** six days : six weeks.
   _____
18. My bus arrived 35 minutes late. If it was due at 9:55 a.m., at what time did it arrive?
   _____
19. The next **prime number** after 17 is _____.
20. A **year** in the **old Roman calendar** consisted of how many months?
   _____

Score:	/20	%	Score:	/20	%

Day 3

1. Evaluate 2^6. _____

2. zero point five + zero point seven =

   _____

3. $3 - 0.05 =$ _____

4. $0.20 \times 0.03 =$ _____

5. $77 \div 0.07 =$ _____

6. A twelve-sided 2-D shape is called a

   _____.

7. Another term for a **circular prism** is a

   _____.

8. If Jack **saves** $4 per week, how much is this per year?

   _____

9. What does $x > 2$ mean? _____

   _____

10. To find the **surface area** of a **prism**, find the area of each face and then _____ them.

11. Find the **area** of the **semicircle**.

    _____

    _____

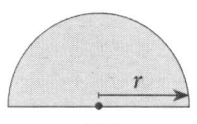

$r = 100\ cm$

12. How many **annuli** can you see?

    _____

13. What **percentage** of 10 is 2.5? _____

14. Simplify $^4/_6$. _____

15. Express the amount MMCCXXII in **Arabic** (common) **numerals**. _____

16. Simplify the **ratio** 0.04 : 0.4. _____

17. Simplify the **ratio** eight days : four weeks. _____

18. **Increase** $500 by 50%. _____

19. The next **prime number** after 19 is _____.

20. If $x = -2$, find the value of $4x - 6$. _____

Day 4

1. Evaluate 2^7. _____

2. zero point one + zero point one one =

   _____

3. $4 - 0.005 =$ _____

4. $0.20 \times 0.002 =$ _____

5. $88 \div 0.08 =$ _____

6. A seven-sided 2-D shape is called a

   _____.

7. How many **faces** does a **cylinder** have? _____

8. If Juanita **saves** $8 per week, how much is this per year? _____

9. What does $x < 2$ mean? _____

   _____

10. What 3-D shape is an Olympic-size pool with a shallow and a deep end?

    _____

11. What is this **shape**?

    (a) an irregular prism
    (b) an irregular pyramid
    (c) an irregular cylinder

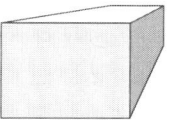

12. Find the area of the trapezoid.

    _____

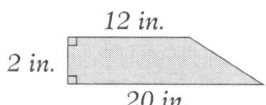

12 in.

2 in.

20 in.

13. What **percentage** of 10 is 5.5? _____

14. Simplify $^8/_{12}$. _____

15. Express the amount MMMX in **Arabic** (common) **numerals**. _____

16. **Ninety-five percent** of one hour is

    _____.

17. Simplify the **ratio** 12 days : 6 weeks. _____

18. **Increase** $2500 by 50%. _____

19. The next **prime number** after 23 is _____.

20. Name the two **months** named in honor of Julius Caesar and Caesar Augustus.

    _____

Day 1

1. Evaluate 2^{-1}. _____

2. zero point two + zero point eight = _____

3. $3 - 0.5 =$ _____   4. $20 \times 0.03 =$ _____

5. $777 \div 0.07 =$ _____

6. How many **vertices** are there on a **hexahedron**? _____

7. Today's date in **international standard** notation is _____ YYYY / _____ MM / _____ DD.

8. If Bec **saves** $190 per week, how much is this per year? _____

9. Show $x > 2$ on the **number line**.

10. The formula to calculate the **perimeter** of a **circle** is

_____.

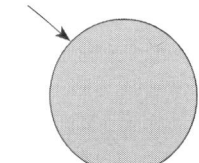

11. The formula to calculate the **circumference** of a **circle** is

_____.

12. Find the **perimeter** of a **triangle** with side lengths of three yards, four yards, and five yards.

_____

13. Write **five minutes to seven in the morning** in short form (digital clock format).

_____

14. **Divide** three by $\frac{1}{3}$. _____

15. Express the amount MMLV in **Arabic** (common) **numerals**. _____

16. Simplify the **ratio** $0.03 : 0.6$. _____

17. Simplify the **ratio** 14 days : 7 weeks. _____

18. The next **prime number** after 3 is _____.

19. The name of our current calendar is the G_____ calendar.

20. Solve for x if $x^2 = 16$. _____

Score: _____ /20   _____ %

Day 2

1. Evaluate 2^{-2}. _____

2. zero point three + zero point eight = _____

3. $4 - 0.6 =$ _____

4. $20 \times 0.02 =$ _____

5. $999 \div 0.09 =$ _____

6. How many **edges** are there on a **hexahedron**? _____

7. What amount of carpet is needed to cover a room 12 meters long and 7 meters wide?

_____

8. If Charlotte **saves** $110 per week, how much is this per year? _____

9. Show $x \geq 2$ on the **number line**.

10. The **volume** of a **prism** is found by multiplying the area of the base by the _____.

11. This **annulus** is the shaded area between two c_____ circles.

12. Find the **circumference** of a circular track with a **radius** of 1 km.

_____

13. Write **five minutes to eight in the morning** in digital clock format._____

14. **Divide** three by $\frac{2}{3}$. _____

15. Express the amount MMLXIX in **Arabic** (common) **numerals**. _____

16. Simplify $\frac{20}{25}$. _____

17. Simplify the **ratio** 1 day : 3 weeks. _____

18. The next **prime number** after two is _____.

19. Who established our current (common) calendar in 1582? _____

20. Solve for x if $x^2 = 25$. _____

Score: _____ /20   _____ %

Day 3

1. Evaluate 2^{-2}. _____

2. zero point eight + zero point six = _____

3. $3 - 0.05 =$ _____

4. $0.20 \times 0.03 =$ _____

5. $7 \div 0.07 =$ _____

6. Are two triangles **congruent** if the side lengths are the same for both **triangles**?

   Yes   No

7. Give an example of an **hexahedron**-shaped object.

   _____

8. If Emma **saves** $130 per week, how much is this per year?

   _____

9. Show $x < 2$ on the **number line**.

10. The v_____ of a **solid** is the amount of space that it occupies.

11. Is this network **traversable**?

    Yes   No

12. Find the value of the **variable** if

    $x + 7 = 3$. _____

13. Write **five minutes to nine in the morning** in short form (digital clock format). _____

14. Increase 50 by 25%. _____

15. Express the amount MMLIII in **Arabic** (common) **numerals**. _____

16. Simplify $x^2 \times x^2$. _____

17. Simplify the **ratio** of two days : three weeks. _____

18. The next **prime number** after 43 is _____.

19. Solve the **inequality** $3x - 2 < 10$.

    _____

20. If $x = 6$, find the value of $4x - 6$. _____

Day 4

1. Evaluate 2^{-4}. _____

2. zero point nine + zero point nine = _____

3. $4 - 0.005 =$ _____

4. $0.20 \times 0.002 =$ _____

5. $9 \div 0.45 =$ _____

6. What abbreviation is used to show **congruency** between two **triangles** with three pairs of sides equal in length?

   _____

7. How many **faces** does a **hexahedron** have? _____

8. If Alan can **save** $175 per week, how much is this per year?

   _____

9. Show $x \leq 2$ on the **number line**.

10. The formula for finding the **area** of a **circle** is _____.

11. Is this network **traversable**?

    Yes   No

    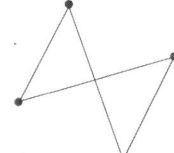

12. Find the value of the **variable** if

    $y + 6 = 4$. _____

13. Write **five minutes to four in the morning** in short form (digital clock format).

    _____

14. Increase 100 by 25%. _____

15. Express the amount MMLIV in **Arabic** (common) **numerals**. _____

16. Simplify $x^2 \times x^5$. _____

17. Simplify the **ratio** ten days : five weeks. _____

18. The next **prime number** after 29 is _____.

19. Solve the **inequality** $30x - 20 < 100$. _____

20. Was the year 1900 a **leap year**?   **Yes   No**

Score: _____ /20 _____ %   **Score:** _____ /20 _____ %

Day 1

1. Evaluate 2^{-3}. _____

2. $450 + 45 =$ _____ 3. $3 - 0.5 =$ _____

4. $20 \times 0.03 =$ _____ 5. $56 \div 0.7 =$ _____

6. What abbreviation is used to show **congruency** between two **triangles** with two pairs of sides equal in length and an angle equal in size?

   _____

7. Write today's date in **international standard** notation.  YYYY / MM / DD

8. If Ned **saves** $45 per week, how much is this per year? _____

9. Show $x > 4$ on the **number line**.

   ```
   ←———————|———————|———————→
           0       4
   ```

10. Using the **metric system**, **area** is measured using units based on the

    s_____ m_____.

11. $(3 + 2 \times 2)^2 =$ _____

12. What is the measure of the **complementary angle** to 60°?

    _____
    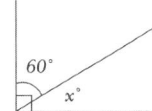
    60°
    x°

13. Write **five minutes to ten in the morning** in short form (digital clock format). _____

14. **Increase** 60 by 20%. _____

15. Express the amount MMXXI in **Arabic (common) numerals**. _____

16. How many years long is a **quadrennium**? _____

17. The **ratio** of a father's age to his son's age is 9 : 2. If the sum of their ages is 55, how old are they each? Father _____ Son _____

18. The next **prime number** after five is _____.

19. Draw a line **parallel** to $\overline{AB}$.

    A •———————————————• B

20. Was the year 2000 a **leap year**?   Yes   No

Day 2

1. Evaluate 2^{-6}. _____

2. $10.56 + 6.79 =$ _____ 3. $4 - 0.6 =$ _____

4. $20 \times 0.02 =$ _____

5. $2500 \div 0.05 =$ _____

6. What abbreviation is used to show **congruency** between two **triangles** with one side equal in length and two angles equal in size?

   _____

7. How long is a **solar year**? _____

8. If Madeline **saves** $65 per week, how much is this per year? _____

9. Show $x \geq 4$ on the **number line**.

   ```
   ←———————|———————|———————→
           0       4
   ```

10. The **volume** of a **solid** is the amount of

    s_____ it holds.

11. $(3 + 2 \times 3)^2 =$ _____

12. What is the measure of the **supplementary angle** to 72°?

    _____
    72°   y°

13. Write **five minutes to one in the morning** in short form (digital clock format). _____

14. **Increase** 50 by 30%. _____

15. Express the amount MMXI in **Arabic (common) numerals**. _____

16. How many of something is a **trilogy**? _____

17. The **ratio** of a father's age to his son's age is 7 : 2. If the sum of their ages is 45, how old are they each? Father = _____ Son = _____

18. The next **prime number** after 59 is _____.

19. Draw a line **perpendicular** to $\overline{AB}$.

    A •———————————————• B

20. Was the year 1800 a **leap year**?   Yes   No

Score: _____ /20 _____ %   Score: _____ /20 _____ %

Day 3

1. Evaluate 2^{-8}. _____
2. zero point four + zero point three = _____
3. $5 - 0.05 =$ _____ 4. $0.20 \times 0.03 =$ _____
5. $7.7 \div 0.07 =$ _____
6. How many cuts are needed to cut a one-meter length of rope into 20 cm pieces? _____
7. The first year of the **twentieth century** was _____.
8. If Leo **saves** $85 per week, how much is this per year? _____
9. What is the cost of four gallons of milk at $2.69 per two gallons? _____
10. The surface of a cylinder is made up of two _____ and a r_____.
11. Is this network **traversable**?

    Yes   No

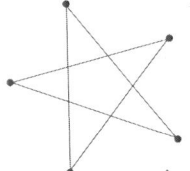

12. Calculate the **angle measure** of $x°$.

    _____

13. Write **five minutes to midnight** in short form (digital clock format). _____
14. $12 \div {}^1\!/_2 =$ _____
15. Express the amount MMMMX in **Arabic** (common) **numerals**. _____
16. Write $33.\overline{3}\%$ as a **fraction** in its simplest form. _____
17. The **ratio** of a mother's age to her son's age is 8 : 2. If the sum of their ages is 50, how old are they each?
    Mother = _____   Son = _____
18. The next **prime number** after 31 is _____.
19. **Similar figures** have the same shape but are different in _____.
20. If $x = 12$, find the value of $4x - 6$. _____

Day 4

1. Evaluate 2^{-4}. _____
2. zero point two + zero point nine = _____
3. $7 - 0.005 =$ _____
4. $0.20 \times 0.002 =$ _____
5. $7.0 \div 0.07 =$ _____
6. How many cuts are needed to cut a one-meter length of rope into 10 cm pieces? _____
7. The first year of the **twenty-first century** was _____.
8. If Johnny saves $55 per week, how much is this per year? _____
9. What is the price of two gallons of orange juice if three gallons **cost** $5.00? _____
10. Prisms are 3-D figures with uniform c_____ f_____.
11. Is this a **traversable** network?

    Yes   No

12. Calculate the **angle measure** of $x°$.

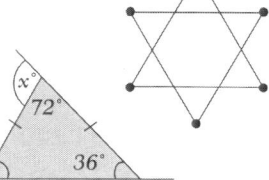

13. Write **five minutes to nine in the evening** in short form (digital clock format). _____
14. **Increase** 50 by 10%. _____
15. Express the amount MMXXIX in **Arabic** (common) **numerals**. _____
16. Write $66^2/_3\%$ as a **fraction** in its simplest form. _____
17. The **ratio** of a father's age to his daughter's age is 6 : 2. If the sum of their ages is 40, how old are they each?
    Father = _____   Daughter = _____
18. The next **prime number** after 41 is _____.
19. What type of **angle** is 120°?
    (a) acute
    (b) obtuse   (c) reflex

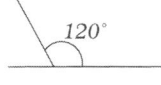

20. Was the year 1700 a **leap year**?   **Yes   No**

Score: _____ /20 _____ %

Score: _____ /20 _____ %

Day 1

1. Evaluate 2^{-1}. _____

2. zero point seven + zero point six = _____

3. $4 - 0.5 =$ _____   4. $90 \times 0.03 =$ _____

5. $7.77 \div 0.07 =$ _____

6. zero point three + zero point nine = _____

7. Today's date in **international standard** notation is ___YYYY___/___MM___/___DD___.

8. If Kevin **saves** $35 per week, how much is this per year? _____

9. If a family buys two gallons of milk per day, how much do they buy in four weeks?

   _____

10. This shape is a c_____ d_____ p_____.

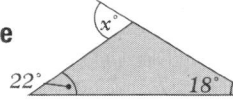

11. How many days are there in 12 consecutive years? _____

12. Calculate the **angle measure** of $x°$. _____

    (triangle with angles $x°$, $22°$, $18°$)

13. Write **five minutes to five in the morning** in short form (digital clock format). _____

14. **Increase** 50 by 20%. _____

15. Express the amount MMXXIV in **Arabic (common) numerals**. _____

16. Write 12.5% as a **fraction** in its simplest form. _____

17. The **ratio** of a mother's age to her daughter's age is 3 : 2. If the sum of their ages is 120, how old are they each?

    Mother _____ Daughter _____

18. The next **prime number** after 101 is _____.

19. What abbreviation is used to show **congruency** between two **triangles** with two pairs of sides equal in length and a right angle in common?

    _____

20. Was the year 1600 a **leap year**?   Yes   No

Day 2

1. Evaluate 2^{-2}. _____

2. zero point five + zero point four = _____

3. $2 - 0.4 =$ _____

4. $200 \times 0.02 =$ _____

5. $8.88 \div 0.08 =$ _____

6. zero point two + zero point seven = _____

7. How many cuts are needed to cut one meter of rope into 50 cm pieces? _____

8. If Harrison saves $15 per week, how much is this per year? _____

9. If a family buys two gallons of milk per day, how much do they buy in a **common year**?

   _____

10. To **convert** an amount from kilometers to meters, just _____ by 1000.

11. How many days are there in 16 consecutive years?

    _____

12. Calculate the **angle measure** of $y°$.

    _____

    (triangle with angles $78°$, $y°$, $32°$)

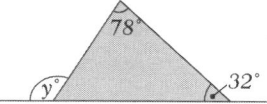

13. $6 - 0.6 =$ _____

14. **Increase** 50 by 40%. _____

15. Express the amount MMXXXVIII in **Arabic (common) numerals**.

16. Write 6.25% as a **fraction** in its simplest form.

    _____

17. The **ratio** of a father's age to his son's age is 4 : 2. If the sum of their ages is 66, how old are they each?
    Father _____ Son _____

18. The next **prime number** after 113 is _____.

19. What abbreviation is used to show **similarity** between two **triangles** where all pairs of angles are common? _____

20. Will the year 2100 be a **leap year**?   Yes   No

Score: /20 %   **Score:** /20 %

Day 3

1. Evaluate 2^{-3}. _____

2. $2.8 + 3.6 =$ _____   3. $3 - 0.05 =$ _____

4. $0.20 \times 0.03 =$ _____   5. $6.66 \div 0.06 =$ _____

6. What set of letters is used to show **congruency** between two **triangles** where all pairs of sides are common? _____

7. How many cuts are needed to divide one meter of rope into 25 cm pieces? _____

8. A box holds six cans in two rows. If each can is 12 cm **tall** and has a **radius** of 4 cm, what are the **dimensions** of the box (in cm)?

_____

9. Show $x \leq 3$ on the **number line**.

$$3$$
←———————|———————→

10. A **trapezoid** has one _____ of parallel sides.

11. How many days are there in four consecutive years? _____

12. The adjective **annual** refers to something occurring once every _____.

13. Write **five minutes to eleven in the morning** in short form (digital clock format).

_____

14. **Increase** 500 by 20%. _____

15. Express the amount MMDLX in **Arabic** (common) **numerals**. _____

16. If a family buys two gallons of milk per **day**, how much do they buy **weekly**? _____

17. The **ratio** of two brothers' ages is 4 : 2. If the sum of their ages is 36, how old are they each?

Older brother _____ Younger brother _____

18. The next **prime number** after 79 is _____.

19. If my bus arrived 55 minutes late and was due at 9:05 a.m., at what time did it arrive? _____

20. If $x = 2$, the value of $4x - 6 =$ _____.

Score: _____ /20 _____ %

Day 4

1. Evaluate 2^{-4}. _____

2. $0.3 + 0.5 =$ _____   3. $4 - 0.005 =$ _____

4. $0.20 \times 0.002 =$ _____

5. $50 \div 0.05 =$ _____

6. What set of letters is used to show **congruency** between two **triangles** where two sides are the same plus one angle is common? _____

7. How many cuts are needed to divide one meter of rope into 20 cm pieces? _____

8. A box holds six cans. If each can is 12 cm **tall** and has a **radius** of 4 cm, what is the **volume** of the box (in cm³)? _____

9. Show $x < 3$ on the **number line**.

$$3$$
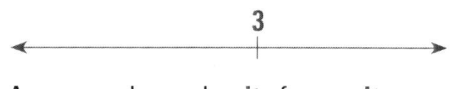

10. A commonly used **unit** of **capacity** is the:
(a) liter.   (b) lire.   (c) lima.

11. How many days are there in eight consecutive years? _____

12. How many years are there in a decade? _____

13. Write **five minutes to eleven in the evening** in digital clock format. _____

14. **Increase** 50 by 5%. _____

15. Express the amount MMMXX in **Arabic** (common) **numerals**. _____

16. If a family buys two gallons of milk per **day**, how much do they buy every **two weeks**?

_____

17. The **ratio** of two sisters' ages is 4 : 2. If the sum of their ages is 24, how old are they each?

Older sister _____ Younger sister _____

18. The next **prime number** after 89 is _____.

19. If my bus arrived 55 minutes late and was due at 9:15 a.m., at what time did it arrive? _____

20. When is the next **leap year**? _____

Score: _____ /20 _____ %

STUDENT RECORD SHEET

Date	Date	Date	Date	Date	Date	Date	Date	Date	Date	Date	Date	Date	Date	Date	Date	Date	Date	Date	Date
Week 1	Week 2	Week 3	Week 4	Week 5	Week 6	Week 7	Week 8	Week 9	Week 10	Week 11	Week 12	Week 13	Week 14	Week 15	Week 16	Week 17	Week 18	Week 19	Week 20
Day 1	Day 1	Day 1	Day 1	Day 1	Day 1	Day 1	Day 1	Day 1	Day 1	Day 1	Day 1	Day 1	Day 1	Day 1	Day 1	Day 1	Day 1	Day 1	Day 1
Day 2	Day 2	Day 2	Day 2	Day 2	Day 2	Day 2	Day 2	Day 2	Day 2	Day 2	Day 2	Day 2	Day 2	Day 2	Day 2	Day 2	Day 2	Day 2	Day 2
Day 3	Day 3	Day 3	Day 3	Day 3	Day 3	Day 3	Day 3	Day 3	Day 3	Day 3	Day 3	Day 3	Day 3	Day 3	Day 3	Day 3	Day 3	Day 3	Day 3
Day 4	Day 4	Day 4	Day 4	Day 4	Day 4	Day 4	Day 4	Day 4	Day 4	Day 4	Day 4	Day 4	Day 4	Day 4	Day 4	Day 4	Day 4	Day 4	Day 4

Date	Date	Date	Date	Date	Date	Date	Date	Date	Date	Date	Date	Date	Date	Date	Date	Date	Date	Date	Date
Week 21	Week 22	Week 23	Week 24	Week 25	Week 26	Week 27	Week 28	Week 29	Week 30	Week 31	Week 32	Week 33	Week 34	Week 35	Week 36	Week 37	Week 38	Week 39	Week 40
Day 1	Day 1	Day 1	Day 1	Day 1	Day 1	Day 1	Day 1	Day 1	Day 1	Day 1	Day 1	Day 1	Day 1	Day 1	Day 1	Day 1	Day 1	Day 1	Day 1
Day 2	Day 2	Day 2	Day 2	Day 2	Day 2	Day 2	Day 2	Day 2	Day 2	Day 2	Day 2	Day 2	Day 2	Day 2	Day 2	Day 2	Day 2	Day 2	Day 2
Day 3	Day 3	Day 3	Day 3	Day 3	Day 3	Day 3	Day 3	Day 3	Day 3	Day 3	Day 3	Day 3	Day 3	Day 3	Day 3	Day 3	Day 3	Day 3	Day 3
Day 4	Day 4	Day 4	Day 4	Day 4	Day 4	Day 4	Day 4	Day 4	Day 4	Day 4	Day 4	Day 4	Day 4	Day 4	Day 4	Day 4	Day 4	Day 4	Day 4